by Maureen Petrosky

ILLUSTRATIONS BY
Liv Lee

Wine Club

A Monthly Guide to Swirling, Sipping, and Pairing with Friends

CHRONICLE BOOKS
SAN FRANCISCO

To Michael, Christopher & Elliot:
Here's to our beautiful life.

And to Mom & Dad:
Thanks for showing us how it's done. Clink!

Library of Congress Cataloging-in-Publication Data available.

ISBN 978-1-7972-2152-6

Manufactured in China.

Illustrations by **LIV LEE**.
Design by **LIZZIE VAUGHAN**.
Typesetting by **TAYLOR ROY**.
Typeset in Adobe Garamond Pro, Faroe, and Neutra Text.

Acacia is a registered trademark of Treasury Wine Estates; Adelsheim is a registered trademark of Adelsheim Vineyard, LLC; Amazon is a registered trademark of Amazon Technologies, Inc.; Archery Summit is a registered trademark of PINE RIDGE WINERY, LLC; Au Bon Climat is a registered trademark of Au Bon Climat LLC; Calera is a registered trademark of DUCKHORN WINE COMPANY; Château Haut-Brion is a registered trademark of SOCIETE CIVILE D'EXPLOITATION AGRICOLE CHATEAU LES CARMES HAUT BRION; Château Lafite Rothschild is a registered trademark of CHATEAU LAFITE ROTHSCHILD; Château Latour is a registered trademark of SOCIETE CIVILE DU VIGNOBLE DE CHATEAU LATOUR; Château Margaux is a registered trademark of SOCIETE CIVILE AGRICOLE CHATEAU MARGAUX; Château Mouton Rothschild is a registered trademark of BARON PHILIPPE DE ROTHSCHILD S.A.; Château Pétrus is a registered trademark of S.C. DU CHATEAU LA FLEUR PETRUS; Clicquot is a registered trademark of MHCS SOCIÉTÉ EN COMMANDITE SIMPLE; Dom Perignon is a registered trademark of Moet Hennessy USA, Inc; Domaine Drouhin is a registered trademark of S. A. MAISON JOSEPH DROUHIN CORPORATION; Dry Farms Wine is a registered trademark of Dry Farm Wines, LLC; Erath Vineyards is a registered trademark of STE. MICHELLE WINE ESTATES LLC; Gary Farrell is a registered trademark of GF Wines, LLC; Goldfish is a registered trademark of PEPPERIDGE FARM, INC; Good Clean Wine is a registered trademark of Good Skin Lifestyle LLC; Google is a registered trademark of Google, Inc.; Heath Bar is a registered trademark of Hershey; Iron Horse is a registered trademark of Iron Horse Vineyards; La Crema is a registered trademark of LC TM HOLDING, LLC; Maldon is a registered trademark of Maldon Crystal Salt Company; Pepperwood Grove is a registered trademark of DON SEBASTIANI & SONS INTERNATIONAL; Rex Hill Vineyards is a registered trademark of A TO Z WINEWORKS, LLC; Rolo is a registered trademark of Société des Produits Nestlé S.A.; Sanford is a registered trademark of Sanford Winery; Sokol Blosser is a registered trademark of Sokol Blosser, Ltd.; Steele is a registered trademark of Shannon Family of Wines; Sure-Jell is a registered trademark of KRAFT FOODS GROUP BRANDS LLC; Sutter Home Winery is a registered trademark of Sutter Home Winery, Inc.; Tantara is a registered trademark of HVP USA LLC; Wine.com is a registered trademark of Wine.com, LLC.

10 9 8 7 6 5 4 3 2 1

Chronicle books and gifts are available at special quantity discounts to corporations, professional associations, literacy programs, and other organizations. For details and discount information, please contact our premiums department at corporatesales@chroniclebooks.com or at 1-800-759-0190.

Chronicle Books LLC
680 Second Street
San Francisco, California 94107
www.chroniclebooks.com

Contents

Welcome to Wine Club!

ONCE UPON A TIME, I graduated from the Culinary Institute of America and passed my sommelier certification with the Master Court of Sommeliers. While I've earned the street cred for sommeliers, the truth is I've learned so much more about wine in my living room than any classroom lecture hall. Like many people, my first wine club started out as a book club. While my friends and I were bonding over wine, it was amazing how much we were learning about it too. That original wine club inspired me to write a book to encourage wine novices and the wine curious to start their own. Let's be honest: book clubs, investment clubs, knitting clubs, whatever you want to call them—we all know they're the perfect excuse to get together with friends, share a drink, and learn something along the way. This year, join me and call it what it is: wine club!

That wine club book kicked off thousands of wine clubs around the country. Since then, I've lived in a couple of different states and worked in a dozen different jobs, all the while hosting and helping friends kick off their own wine clubs. I've learned a lot about what works and what doesn't, and now you get the foolproof scoop on how to create a fabulous wine club of your own. There is power in gathering for wine club, and this year you'll see it can also be a place where you cultivate meaningful friendships or network if you like, all while enjoying the best-tasting therapy around.

This book is not going to make you a world-class sommelier or in-depth wine expert. What it will do is break down any fear factors surrounding wine, so that you can branch out, discover what you like to drink, and have some great food and fun along the way.

Elements of a Great Wine Club

If you have some wineglasses, a bottle opener, some foil, and a few friends, then voilà: You have a wine club! There is no need for prior wine experience or training to have a wine club—novices and experts alike can follow along as I guide you through new grapes or styles of wine each month. The book is organized by the calendar year, with wine picks and food pairings to go with the seasons of the northern hemisphere. But consider these merely suggestions; if you feel like starting with the Chardonnay chapter instead of Cabernet Sauvignon, go right ahead—this is *your* wine club.

Because I don't want you sipping on an empty stomach, each chapter also has a few simple but sophisticated, throw-together or make-ahead snack and appetizer recipes that will enhance your wine-tasting experience. As with a book club, make sure to take turns hosting! Wine club works best when you share the responsibilities of bringing wine and appetizers each month.

Now get your drinking shoes on—it's time to kick off your wine club!

The Guest List

My number one rule for wine club is only drink with people you like! Once you mention a wine club, people will come out of the woodwork to join. So, I recommend you keep it under wraps until you've done your due diligence. You really want to cap the guest list at ten to twelve people, tops. (I prefer even fewer, if possible.) A big get-together is great, but beware: The more members, the more you will find it difficult to focus on the wine. I'm certainly not one to discourage a good soiree, but if you want the focus of your club to be learning a little about wine, then save the big guest list for a bar meetup or cocktail party.

As for choosing which mates to toast, keep proximity in mind. If you live in a locale that allows all members to take public transportation, then this factor is less important. But for clubs that may be meeting in, say, the suburbs, make sure you're all within range of a car service or simply take turns as the designated driver.

The Wine

Wine may be daunting at first, but with baby steps (or baby *sips*, as I like to call them), you'll be up and running in no time. Each chapter is devoted to a different style of wine (like Champagne) or varietal (wine made from a specific grape, such as Pinot Noir or Cabernet Sauvignon). We'll start off with some wines that you may be familiar with and move on to some I hope you've never heard of. There are literally thousands of wines out there, so in order to actually learn something each month, I decided to pare it down to the most popular or most widely available. Each month, you'll only taste test five or six wines from that month's category.

The host should assign each wine selection to a guest to purchase and bring to that month's wine club. Whenever you do a wine tasting, there will always be some wines that are more expensive than others. For example, whoever brings a traditional French Champagne will surely shell out more dough than the person assigned to bring the Spanish Cava. Work this out among your friends, perhaps with a rotating schedule of who will buy the most expensive wine each month. Or let two wine club members pitch in on the month's most expensive pick. Keep it fair—you don't want to start the club off with any hard feelings!

The host should make a list of the names and numbers of the bottles to keep track but only reveal them once the tasting is completed. Encourage guests to bring their assigned bottles wrapped in foil or in a brown bag and marked with the number you assign them. If you use aluminum foil, make sure the foil goes under the bottle as well so it won't slip off when pouring. In addition, be sure to remove the entire foil capsule that covers the cork or the screw cap at the top of the bottle so there are no signs of what lies beneath. The retail prices are also to be revealed when the bottles are uncovered at the end of the tasting.

If you can't see the name or the price, you are more likely to taste true to your palate and not be swayed. Even master sommeliers have been tricked! By covering the bottles, you learn to trust yourself and be confident in sipping, which will help you when you're eventually shopping for what you like.

The Glassware

I recommend using all-purpose glassware (and don't be afraid to ask your friends to bring some if you don't have enough). You can serve your wine in any glass you have on hand, but avoid serving in ceramic mugs or plastic or paper cups when possible.

Very few months will require specific glassware, save for two notable exceptions:

ACRYLIC GLASSWARE For outdoor wine clubs, you have the option to use acrylic glassware (this does not mean plastic tumblers you normally use for drinking soda—those can be porous and carry odd flavors from dishwashing soap). Acrylic glasses look sleek and are safer than glass if you're sipping poolside. The biggest difference between glassware and these acrylic wineglass alternatives is the weight; I also find that my wine does not stay cool as long as it does in a wineglass.

CHAMPAGNE GLASSWARE There are lots of styles of Champagne glasses out there—the coupe, the trumpet glass, the flute, and the tulip—so I'll leave it to you to choose your favorite (see page 267)!

Not everything should go in the dishwasher, especially your glassware for bubbly. Don't believe me? Try this little test: Wash one flute in the dishwasher and another by hand. Now, pour one of your favorite sparkling wines in that hand-washed glass. Oh, that's beautiful! Okay, now try your sparkler in the machine-washed glass. Oh, that's . . . weird. What happened to the bubbles? That's right—once you taste what residual soap does to your sparkling wine's bubbles and body, you'll never put your glasses in the dishwasher again.

Another tip is to dry glassware with paper towels, not dish towels. Using a dish towel can leave your sparkling wines, especially, looking a little flat. The culprit? Fabric softener and teensy particles of lint.

Moral of the story? Hand-wash and hand-dry your glassware with paper towels or lint-free cloths.

When It's Your Turn to Host

As with a book club, I suggest all wine club members take turns hosting the gathering. Here's what to do when it's your turn to host.

PLAN AHEAD. I recommend reading that month's chapter two weeks in advance. This will give you enough time to assign wines and appetizers to guests, and to start preparing little by little for your get-together.

ASSIGN THE WINES AND APPETIZERS. Keep in mind that some months the wines may range in price, so if one wine is significantly higher-priced, split it between two members. On average, wine club members should be prepared to spend $20 to $30 per month on wine or food. If you live in an area with wine delivery, another option would be to schedule wine to be delivered to the host with guests chipping in via a payment app.

PREPARE THE FOOD. Every recipe in this book has steps that can be done ahead of time, so you can shop a week in advance for supplies. The more you do in advance, the more you can enjoy time with your guests.

CONDUCT THE TASTING. All tastings should be conducted blind, as mentioned earlier. The reveal of all the bottles can be conducted once all the guests have had a chance to taste each wine. See How to Evaluate Each Wine on page 13 for more guidance.

Some Ground Rules

- Be sure to have your designated driver or mode of safe transportation home in place before you start the evening. Leaving this task until late in the night will prove to be a bad idea.
- Follow the one-to-one rule: One glass of water for each glass of wine.
- Don't drink on an empty stomach—always have a little nibble before you start taste testing.
- You must commit to trying all of the wines being evaluated.

TIPS FOR TASTEFUL TASTINGS

Here are a few tips to make sure your tastings go off without a hitch:

— Remember, you only taste test, sip, and sniff the first go-round, so a 1 to 2 oz [30 to 60 ml] pour is sufficient. If you pour more than that, your guests will end up swirling that wine right out of their glasses.

— Use darker tablecloths (or none at all) for a red wine tasting to avoid staining your linens. If you do go this route, however, pass out white sheets of paper so guests can hold their glasses up to something white to see the real color of the wine.

— When pouring, turn the bottle slightly as you finish the pour; this will prevent too much dripping. Have a napkin in one hand to catch any drips. Also, there's no need to show off your aim and pour the wine from a mile above. You'll splash it, and that's not cool if it hits someone's clothes.

— Spit buckets are just about as dainty as they sound, but it's recommended that you spit after you swish the wine around your palate when tasting wines for learning purposes. This way you aren't influenced by your alcohol intake. I suggest passing out individual opaque-colored glasses or plastic cups so tasters can keep their spit to themselves.

— You should also cleanse the palate, and rinse the glass, with water in between each wine.

- You must wait until you have tasted and talked about each wine before pouring yourself a grown-up size of your favorite wine from the lineup.
- Avoid wearing perfumed products. This will interfere with your ability to experience the wine's tastes and aromas.

How to Evaluate Each Wine

Once you're settled and ready to begin the tasting, pass out writing implements and paper to note your findings.

What Do You See?

First impressions can tell you a lot about what you are about to taste. Pay attention to the appearance—not just the color, but the depth of color as well. Right off the bat, you'll see whether it's white, red, or rosé colored. The best way to see your wine is to hold it against a white piece of paper or against a white tablecloth under sufficient light. (Wine club is not the time to dim the lights for ambience.) In each chapter you will see notes for what you should be looking for, from color, viscosity, and, of course, bubbles.

Be Nose-y

The art of swirling and sniffing is simple. There are some techniques to help you start smelling past the alcohol and get to the good stuff. For example, if a wine's label says it smells like blueberries, open a jar of blueberry jam and have it on the table so everyone can smell it. Then, smell the wine to see whether you can detect the same notes.

Sometimes, people can't smell anything, especially after sniffing a lot of wine. This is called nasal fatigue. The simplest way to fix that is to smell something different, like your hand or your hair. Sounds weird, but you'll see it works. There is no right or wrong thing to smell. Although I'll provide different scent notes for each wine, if you think a wine smells like something I haven't listed, go with it. Smell can be subjective for each person, but I encourage you to share your thoughts out loud even if you think they're out of the box—you may be surprised when others agree with you.

What Are You Tasting?

The easiest way to taste what's in the glass is to associate it with flavors you already know. We'll explore flavors from lemon to chocolate to tobacco and vanilla. Each chapter, I'll share with you the most common flavors typical of that month's wine.

What Is Body?

Most people have experienced different varieties of milk, which is why I use it as a comparison when you're learning the difference between light-, medium-, and full-bodied wines: Fat-free milk is light-bodied, whole milk is medium-bodied, and cream is full-bodied. For example, if your wine is more like fat-free milk—watery, thin, and doesn't leave a coating on your mouth—then it's light-bodied.

Finishing School

Every wine has a finish. Take a sip, swallow, and start counting to yourself. If immediately after you swallow there is no lasting taste or mouthfeel from your wine, then it has a short finish. If you get to the count of five and still have some lingering effects, that's a medium finish. If you can carry on a conversation and still feel your mouth puckering or taste the wine you sipped minutes later, then that is a long finish. Each month, I'll discuss the difference between the long and short of it.

Food and Wine Pairing

The only way to learn about which wines go well with which foods is through trial and error. Take a sip, then take a bite. Take a bite, then take a sip. Take a sip and a bite at the same time. Take note of the changes in your mouth. I'll make suggestions, but only you know what you like and dislike. Here are three ways to pair food and wine like an expert:

- **BRIDGING** Using the wine you're drinking as an ingredient in the dish you're eating.

- **COMPLEMENTING** Serving a wine that is full-bodied with a rich dish, like a Cabernet Sauvignon with a juicy steak.
- **CONTRASTING** Serving a wine that contrasts with the elements of the dish. For example, if your dish features a rich cream sauce, then serve a light, bubbly wine to cut through the fat.

Get Your Drink On

Each guest should bring along a small bound notebook or wine journal (or in absence of that, even the notes app on your phone will do). It keeps you organized, and with all your notes in one place you can easily refer to them on your next trip to the wine shop. Before you know it, your wine notebook will become more like a diary full of funny stories and wine notes you'll cherish.

Just like the pros, we will evaluate each of the following categories for each wine:

Tasting Date:	Wine #:
Type of Wine:	
Vintage:	
Color:	
Aroma:	
Taste:	
Body:	
Finish:	
Food Pairing:	
Price Value:	

Cabernet Sauvignon

Welcome to wine club! We'll kick off this year by sipping and swirling a big red wine: Cabernet Sauvignon. Often called "Cab" for short, this full-bodied, rich pour is the most widely available and popular wine in the world. If you've ever ordered the house red, chances are you've tasted a Cab or two. This month, you'll taste your way through Cabs from Argentina, France, and California until you find the perfect one for you.

Getting to Know Cab

Let's start with some basics: Who makes up all these names for wine? Very often, wines from Europe are named for the region or towns in which they're made. For instance, Champagne is named for the Champagne region in northern France. Outside of Europe, most wine-growing regions keep it simple and name the wine for the grapes from which they're made. These are called "varietals" (it's easy to remember—just think grape variety). Cabernet Sauvignon is named for the Cabernet Sauvignon grape (or varietal), Merlot is named for the Merlot grape, Chardonnay is—you guessed it—the name of a grape.

Cabernet Sauvignon grapes can grow just about anywhere, which is why this wine type is so popular and widely available. It originally hails from France's Bordeaux region (many of the famous wines of this region are based on Cabernet Sauvignon grapes), but many other regions around the world have established themselves as Cabernet epicenters. California's Napa Valley has been called the King of Cab, with certain pours earning top honors, even by the French. Argentina, Chile, and Australia are particularly well known for great Cabs, and South Africa is right on their heels. This grape has even spread east into China!

Legends of Bordeaux

There are a ton of wines from France—so many you could spend a lifetime learning about them. Because we only have a month, we'll focus on the Left Bank of the Bordeaux region, where Cabernet Sauvignon dominates in the blends. Here, you need to know the producer—or in this case, château (the name of a wine estate)—from the region to be sure you're getting Cabernet Sauvignon. Be prepared: You'll also spend more for these bottles, but it's worth it to learn the importance of the Old World style (see page 25).

The most famous, and usually most expensive, wines come from these top five châteaux in Bordeaux: Château Latour, Château Mouton

Rothschild, Château Lafite Rothschild, Château Haut-Brion, and Château Margaux. There are plenty of estates beyond these in this region, so I suggest you start with something more moderate in price while you're still figuring out whether this style is right for you. Lower-priced wines from this region will still give you a good idea of the Bordeaux style. Just beware of basic Bordeaux with no village name—wine that only says the word "Bordeaux" on the label—as these are not single estate and not made with the same standards as the château wines. When in doubt, ask your wine merchant before you buy.

Terroir's Not So Terrifying...

The word *terroir* (*ter-WAHR*) is a little awkward to spit out, but the concept is important to dig into as we move forward and learn more about wine. Because there is no direct English translation, we use this fancy French word to describe all of the influences on a vine, including soil, climate, wind, etc. Wines made from vines grown in a particular place will—year after year—show distinctive elements of its terroir in the glass. So, a Merlot from Pomerol will always be identifiable and different from a Merlot from the Languedoc region, because of its terroir.

I know it's a bit abstract to grasp, but as you continue to taste and sniff, try to take note of what you smell. Is it earthy or fruit-forward? If it's earthy in aroma, you're more than likely swirling an Old World wine, and if it's fruit-forward you'll be sipping something from the New World.

Vintage Matters—or Does It?

Vintage is the year the grapes were harvested/picked. Champagnes and Port wine are nonvintage; that is, they're made of a blend of wines from grapes harvested from different years. That's why you don't see a date on those bottles. On the other hand, still wines (ones without bubbles) are almost always labeled with the year the grapes were harvested. What does the year matter to what's in the bottle—and in the glass?

It can matter a lot. If the growing season is too hot, the grapes shrivel up like raisins, leaving little juice and more overripe fruit flavors and aromas. On the other hand, too much rain can plump up volume and dilute flavors and body. Grapes drowned by a sudden rainfall can burst, causing them to rot. Think of weather as a "Goldilocks" deal: It can't be too hot, too wet, or too dry. For a great vintage, it needs to be just right.

Vintage also matters because wines change as they age, that is, how long they sit after they've been harvested. For example, in a young red Cab (one that is harvested, bottled, and released right away), alcohol can be the first thing you taste and smell. With time in a barrel or in the bottle, that harsh heat you experience in your mouth from the alcohol mellows out. This allows all the flavors to meld together and create a more balanced wine.

Also, those in-your-face tannins in young red wines that make your mouth pucker like a fish will actually soften over the years, rounding out the mouthfeel and balance of the wine. Because Cabernet Sauvignon has lots of tannins, it's often suggested that they hang out a while in the bottle before drinking. If you don't have all that time, you can decant a wine (see page 24).

When buying a Cab for your tasting, you might want to ask your wine merchant for one that's ready to drink now, which usually will prove to be a couple years older than the year you're shopping.

Taking Flight

Even wine professionals don't all agree on the importance of vintage. Some believe that variation from year to year is less important than variation from producer to producer, or the age of the bottle, and even more so, the price. For example, a $65 2019 Napa Cab is a world away

TANNIN TALK

Now that we're talking Cab, this is the perfect time to tell you about tannins, because Cabernet Sauvignon is full of them. When you sip a red wine and you are left with a dry feeling on the roof or sides of your mouth, those are the tannins at work (or shall we say play?). The sensation is similar to the feeling you get if you drink a very strong cup of tea.

Tannins come from the seeds, stems, and skins of the grapes and the oak barrels used to age wine. In young red wine, the tannins can be very strong and astringent, but as the wine ages, the tannins soften and round out. Tannins give structure to red wines, along with added sensations as you sip; they are a large part of the personality of big reds, and what make red wines so perfect for pairing with heavier foods like steak, creamy cheeses, and even rich desserts.

Ever pour out the last sips from a bottle only to find clumps of dark purple or brown sediment plunk into your glass? Those are from tannins too. As wine ages, tannins clump together, and along with the pigments (those gorgeous shade of red) and tartrates (small little crystals you'll sometimes see on the bottom of a cork or in your wine, a.k.a. "wine diamonds") in the wine, they form a sediment that settles to the bottom or side of the bottle. It happens in red wines mostly, but it can happen in older oak-aged whites (like the Chardonnay in chapter 3) too.

from a $10 2020 California Cab. Only a few people in the world can truly tell the difference between a $10 Cab from 2000 and one from 2001. Again, it's not the year that's going to make or break anything. If you don't like a 2017 Chianti, you probably won't like a 2020 Chianti.

A fun way to test this for yourself is to try a flight of wine. Buy three Cabs from the same producer from different vintages and taste them side by side (also known as a "flight" of wine). See whether you can tell any major differences and whether the price of each reflects any flaws, such as an off year weather-wise.

Wine Speak

BALANCED This term describes a wine in which the sugar, acidity, fruit, tannin, alcohol, and wood are all present without hiding or dominating each other.

BIG This term is used for wine that fills your taste buds with big flavors, your nose with big aromas, and your mouth with full body. These wines hold their own when paired with heavy foods and are too big to pair with delicacies of the sea. Cab, Zinfandel, and Syrah are the ringleaders in the "big wine" arena, and depending on the winemaker, sometimes Merlot can even be a big wine too.

DECANTING WINE To do this, simply pour the wine from the bottle into a decanter; this lets the wine breathe and allows some of that alcohol scent to blow off. If you're decanting to remove the sediment, stop pouring when the sediment from the bottom of the bottle reaches the bottle's neck—the idea is to leave the sediment in the bottle—or pour through cheesecloth into the decanter. Unless you're feeling fancy, there's no need for a crystal decanter—you can use a glass carafe or just pour that wine right into a big glass bowl!

LETTING WINE "BREATHE" You'll often hear people suggest opening a bottle of red well before it's poured so it can "breathe." This means exposing wine to air by decanting it or swirling it in a glass to blow off some of the alcohol and truly show off its aromas and characteristics. This is especially important for high-alcohol wines like Cabs and Zinfandels, and it helps young red wines "open up" and show you what the future may hold once they have been aged.

NEW WORLD WINE This is a general term for wines produced in the Americas, Australia, New Zealand, and South Africa—basically, anywhere but Europe. Cabs from California? New World. New World wines more often take advantage of science and technology when planting vines and making wine. New World winemakers can and do change their style on a dime, and they don't rely on terroir to guide them. These wines are mostly made to be drunk immediately upon release.

OLD WORLD WINE This is a general term for wines produced in Europe. Cabs from Bordeaux? Old World. Old World, like old school, means steeped in tradition. Old World wineries depend on Mother Nature to guide them, and many Old World wines need a little age to gain their grace and beauty.

January's Picks

For your wine club's Cabernet Sauvignon tasting, the host should assign five Cabernet Sauvignons from five different parts of the world. This may take a little coordinating, so give your guests some notice. No need to obsess over the year on the label. What we're aiming to find out this month is if you like Cabernet Sauvignon, and if so, which area of the world is pouring up your fave.

Like I said earlier, this grape grows all over the place, but here are a few easy-to-find wines you can pick for your tasting:

Napa Valley, California   ($15 to $25)

Hold on to your seat because these juicy reds come in a variety of gorgeous ruby to purple hues and serve up sips that are intensely tannic, jammy, and accented with oak. They are widely available and can range in price from $15 to well over $100 a bottle. Plan to spend around $20 on this bottle for the tasting.

Washington State   ($15 to $20)

Cabs from Washington State are known for their ripe fruit flavors but tend to have lighter tannins than their Californian cousins.

Bordeaux, France   ($30 to $40)

Now we're getting fancy with French Cabs that show finesse and are more reserved in their personality than American Cabernets. While they certainly have fruit flavors, they also have earthier aromas, such as wet rocks or mineral flavors, woven into the juice. Red wines from Bordeaux are always blended (made from more than one grape), usually from Cabernet Sauvignon and Merlot. This is when a little geography comes in handy. The Bordeaux region has three top-producing areas: the Left Bank, the Right Bank, and Graves. However, you probably won't see "Left Bank" or "Right Bank" on a label—instead, you'll see the château or producer. (Note that you may run across "Graves" on labels in this section of your wine shop, because Graves is a named region within Bordeaux.) This month, we're aiming to include something from the Left Bank, where the wines are made predominantly with Cab, including châteaus located in Margaux, St-Julien, Pauillac, Haut-Médoc, or St-Estèphe. Remember, look for something from Bordeaux with a village name on the label to get a true sense of this style of Cab.

Chile   ($15 to $20)

Chile is flush with Cabernet Sauvignon. Influenced by both Old and New World styles, the wines vary in intensity and sophistication. One thing for sure is that they have all the classic Cab attributes of red and black fruits (black cherries, currants, even fig) and tannins, but also that unmistakable green bell pepper. You can find great deals on decadent Cabs from regions like Aconcagua, Cachapoal, Colchagua, and Maipo.

Argentina   ($15 to $20)

You may be more familiar with Argentina's other darling red, Malbec, but this South American spot, like Chile, is also serving up Cabs for a steal. Look for pours from Mendoza, its largest growing region, for a great addition to this month's lineup of wines.

South Africa   ($15 to $25)

These guys might be a little more difficult to locate, but if you can score one from the Stellenbosch, Paarl, or Robertson regions for your tasting, don't miss the chance. I suggest you call your wine shop ahead of time and ask if they carry it or if they can order you one.

Australia ($15 to $25)

There is *a lot* of great Cab flowing from Down Under. Most of these will be more your New World style: fruit-forward and easy drinking. They tend not to be as in-your-face as the California Cabs, but still you'll get fruit first when sipping. Some spots to seek out include the Barossa Valley, McLaren Vale, Langhorne Creek, Margaret River, Coonawarra, and the Yarra Valley.

Ringer: Merlot from California ($15 to $20)

This month, throw in a Merlot as a ringer, and see who can guess which bottle it is. Here's a hint: The Merlot should be noticeably lighter in color than the Cabs. The Merlot will also be lighter and softer on the palate.

Get Your Drink On

Get those tasting sheets ready—we're finally going to start sipping some of this stuff. Cabs are sure to warm you up and make your cheeks rosy—red wines have a funny way of doing that. Take your time and reflect on all the things you see, smell, taste, and feel.

TIME AND TEMP

If you purchased a bottle of Cab, more than likely it is ready to be enjoyed now. While an expiration date would be helpful, this red is typically ready three to five years after it was harvested. That's easy to determine by the vintage date, which is the year on the label. The aging has already been done in the barrels and bottles, and it is released when they think it's at its best. You can cellar, a.k.a. store or put away, Cabernet for years, as long as you have the proper storage conditions and understand the wine will change with time, mellowing its fruit and lessening its structure.

Cabernet Sauvignon should be enjoyed a little cooler than the average home temperature. If your thermostat sits above 70°F [21°C], pop your Cab in the fridge for 15 to 20 minutes before your pour. The ideal sipping temperature for this smooth red wine is between 60°F and 65°F [15.5°C and 18.3°C]. If it's too warm, you'll get lots of alcohol and won't get the clear fruit flavors. If it's too cold, you won't be able to identify the flavors and aromas at all. As with other big reds, once you've removed the cork, the life of that wine is two to four days.

COLOR Cabernet Sauvignon hues range from dark red to ruby red to purplish red. While young Cabs will have vibrant red hues, a twenty-year-old bottle of Cabernet Sauvignon may appear more translucent, be lighter in color, and have brownish hues. You should never use the term watery to describe a Cab—if what you have in the glass is watery, I'd be skeptical that it's truly a Cab. What you're looking at should be deep, dark, and rich in color.

AROMA If you're tasting Cabs from California, the wines in your glass will most likely smell fruitier than if you're tasting those from Bordeaux. Some fruits you may smell are black cherries, black currants, and cassis. Cabs can also be vegetal and smell of asparagus or red bell pepper. Other aromas to look for are vanilla, clove, black pepper, cocoa, and even licorice. See whether you can detect these other elements as you inhale: eucalyptus, mint, and chocolate (milk or dark). Share out loud with your fellow tasters any other aromas that come to mind. It's likely you're not the only one. Remember, the longer the wine is exposed to the air (a.k.a. open) the more the aromas will change.

TASTE Cabernet Sauvignon is a big wine that's luscious and takes over in your mouth. As you sip, notice its big aromas, big flavor, big body—and big alcohol. The alcohol in Cabernet Sauvignon can range from 12 percent to over 14 percent (check out the label—it will tell you the alcohol content). If at first you smell and taste only the alcohol, let the wine breathe before retasting.

BODY I have never had a Cabernet Sauvignon that wasn't medium- to full-bodied. This grape makes a big impression with a big, juicy, full body that comes from the tannins in the grape's thick skin and the aging in oak vats. If you liken it to milk, Cab usually falls somewhere around whole milk in the spectrum. As you sip Cabs this month, notice the tannins and how you experience them. If your mouth feels like cotton after you sip a big red wine, that means the tannins are very strong; if you just slightly feel that dryness in your cheeks or across the roof of your mouth, then the tannins are soft.

FINISH Sticking with the "big" theme, Cabs usually have a big finish. Whether it's a burning throat from the high alcohol or you feel like you have cotton mouth from the tannins, you are sure to know you just sipped a Cab. Take note of how many seconds these feelings linger. A well-balanced Cab will leave your mouth feeling like you want another sip, not like you need a glass of water.

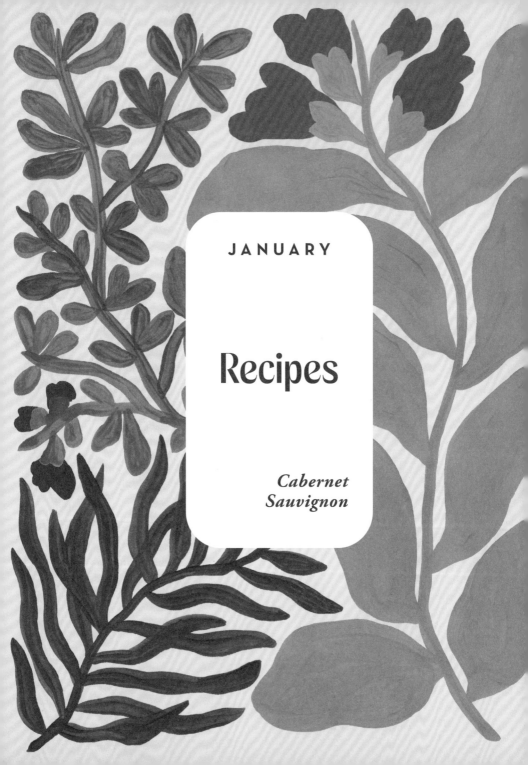

JANUARY

Recipes

Cabernet
Sauvignon

LET'S EAT This month, we're complementing our big reds with rich bites like creamy Brie and bold flavors like bacon and Japanese barbecue. Note that spicy food is a big no-no when drinking Cab! You see, big reds like Cabernet Sauvignon are usually higher in alcohol. On its own, higher alcohol produces heat, and when you pair it with spicy food, you're adding fuel to the fire. So come hungry for some great grub and get cozy with Cabs for this wine club month.

Baked brie is one of the most rewarding and simplest appetizers to assemble. It does double duty as a centerpiece and a delicious, warm gooey treat. If cherry isn't your favorite, you can try raspberry, currant, or strawberry jam here instead.

Baked Brie with Balsamic Cherries and Sage

SERVES 12 TO 14

¹/₂ cup [80 g] cherry preserves

2 Tbsp balsamic glaze (see Note)

1 sheet puff pastry, thawed

One 4 in [10 cm] round of Brie, about 8 oz [230 g]

2 tsp chopped fresh sage

1 egg, beaten

Crackers, for serving

Preheat the oven to 400°F [200°C]. Line a baking sheet with parchment paper.

In a small bowl, stir the cherry preserves and balsamic glaze together until evenly combined.

Unfold the sheet of puff pastry and place the round of Brie in the center. Top the Brie with the cherry preserves mixture. Sprinkle the sage on top.

Fold the puff pastry up and over the Brie. Using a pastry brush, coat the entire pastry with the beaten egg. Place on the prepared baking sheet seam side up.

Bake for 35 to 40 minutes, until golden brown. Transfer to a serving platter and serve with crackers.

Note: Balsamic glaze is simply balsamic vinegar that has been reduced by half to the consistency of molasses. Either use store-bought glaze or make your own.

Often, Marcona almonds come already roasted and salted. If that's all you can find in your store, simply add the fresh herbs and warm through to bring out the flavors.

MAKES ABOUT 1½ CUPS [230 G]

8 oz [230 g] roasted plain Marcona almonds

1 tsp olive oil

1 tsp fresh thyme leaves

1 tsp chopped fresh rosemary

2 tsp fleur de sel

Marcona Almonds with Herbs and Fleur de Sel

Preheat the oven to 350°F [180°C].

Place the almonds on an unlined baking sheet. Drizzle with the olive oil and sprinkle with the thyme and rosemary. Toss to evenly coat. Bake for 10 minutes, until lightly toasted and aromatic.

Remove from the oven and sprinkle with almost all of the fleur de sel to coat evenly. Pour into a bowl and sprinkle the remaining salt on top. Serve warm.

The red wine with red meat pairing is a no-brainer. If you don't want to make your own, premade Japanese barbecue sauce can be found in the Asian section of grocery stores, specialty shops, or online. It's a great condiment to keep on hand for quick and easy marinades and dipping sauces as well. You will need twenty-four 10 in [25 cm] skewers for this recipe.

Japanese BBQ Beef Skewers (Yakiniku)

Place the sliced beef and ¼ cup [60 ml] of sauce into a zip-top bag. Make sure the beef is completely coated with the sauce. Place the bag in the fridge for at least two hours or up to overnight (8 hours).

Remove the beef and thread one slice onto each skewer. Place the beef skewers on a foil-lined baking sheet. Cover the exposed part of the skewers with foil.

Preheat the oven to a full broil.

Place the baking sheet on the top shelf of the oven and broil for 2 minutes. Turn the skewers over, re-cover the exposed part of the skewers with foil, and broil for 2 more minutes on the other side.

MAKES 20 TO 24 SKEWERS

1 lb [455 g] skirt steak, sliced thinly against the grain in ¼ in [6 mm] slices

½ cup [120 ml] Japanese BBQ sauce (recipe follows)

¼ cup [20 g] sliced green onions

¼ cup [8 g] fresh cilantro leaves

Remove and serve on a plate or platter with the remaining ¼ cup [60 ml] of Japanese BBQ sauce in a small ramekin for dipping. Sprinkle the skewers with the green onions and cilantro leaves for garnish and serve.

**MAKES 1½ CUPS
[360 ML]**

3 garlic cloves, minced

6 Tbsp [90 ml] sake

6 Tbsp [90 ml] mirin

6 Tbsp [90 ml] soy sauce

¼ cup [50 g] sugar

3 Tbsp sesame oil

Japanese BBQ Sauce

In a small saucepan, bring the garlic, sake, mirin, and soy sauce to a simmer for 3 minutes. Add the sugar and stir until dissolved. Remove from the heat, strain into a small bowl, and add the sesame oil. Refrigerate until ready to use.

This jam is addictive. Served with pimento cheese, a southern staple, on a sliced baguette, it works great with red wine, especially Cabernet Sauvignon.

Bacon–Red Wine Jam and Pimento Cheese Crostini

MAKES 10 TO 12 CROSTINI

1 lb [455 g] bacon, cut into $\frac{1}{2}$ in [13 mm] pieces

1 medium onion, finely diced

2 garlic cloves, minced

$\frac{1}{4}$ cup [60 ml] red wine

$\frac{1}{2}$ cup [120 ml] brewed coffee

$\frac{1}{4}$ cup [60 ml] apple cider vinegar

$\frac{1}{3}$ cup [65 g] dark brown sugar

$\frac{1}{3}$ cup [80 ml] maple syrup

$\frac{1}{4}$ cup [30 g] minced fresh jalapeño

Salt and freshly ground black pepper

$\frac{1}{2}$ slender baguette, cut on the bias into $\frac{1}{4}$ to $\frac{1}{2}$ in [6 to 13 mm] slices

Bacon Jam

In a large sauté pan over medium heat, cook the bacon until the fat is rendered and it is beginning to brown, 12 to 14 minutes. Remove the bacon from the pan and set aside on a paper towel–lined plate.

Pour off all but 1 Tbsp of the fat, lower the heat to medium, and add the onion and garlic to the pan. Cook until they are soft and translucent, 6 to 8 minutes.

Add the red wine, coffee, vinegar, brown sugar, maple syrup, and jalapeño to the pan. Bring to a boil and cook for 2 to 3 minutes.

Add the bacon back in and stir to combine. Simmer slowly over low heat with the lid off for about 45 minutes, or until the liquid has a syrupy consistency. Taste and add salt and pepper if necessary. Store the leftovers in an airtight container in the refrigerator. Bring to room temperature or slightly reheat before serving.

One 4 oz [115 g] block good yellow Cheddar cheese, grated (see Note)

1 Tbsp grated yellow onion

1½ Tbsp minced pimento or roasted red bell pepper

3 Tbsp mayonnaise

Salt

Note: It is important to use freshly grated cheese, as using bagged pre-shredded cheese will affect the consistency.

Pimento Cheese

In the bowl of a food processor, place the grated cheese, onion, pimento, and mayonnaise and purée until the desired consistency is reach. Season with salt. Scrape into a serving bowl, cover with plastic wrap, and chill until ready to serve.

To assemble: Spread about 2 tsp of pimento cheese on each slice of bread and then top with ½ to 1 tsp of bacon jam. Serve immediately.

Think of this as the best chocolate-covered pretzel you'll ever have. With all the chocolate, dark cocoa, and coffee aromas in Cabs, this dessert is perfect for January's wine club.

Three-Ingredient Dark Chocolate Mousse with Coffee Whip and Pretzels

SERVES 8 TO 10

Mousse

10 oz [280 g] dark chocolate chips

2 cups [480 ml] heavy cream

¼ cup [30 g] confectioners' sugar

Coffee Whip

¼ cup [30 g] instant coffee granules

¼ cup [50 g] granulated sugar

¼ cup [60 ml] boiling water

24 to 30 mini pretzels

To make the mousse: Place the chocolate chips in a heatproof bowl.

In a small saucepan over medium heat, bring 1 cup [240 ml] of the cream just to a simmer. Pour over the chocolate chips and stir to melt.

In another bowl, add the remaining 1 cup [240 ml] of cream and the confectioners' sugar. Using a handheld mixer on medium-high speed, beat until medium peaks form.

Using a rubber spatula, gently fold the whipped cream into the chocolate mixture in three batches.

Once fully incorporated, spoon the mixture into eight to ten small ramekins, filling each halfway. Place in the refrigerator.

To make the coffee whip: In a mixing bowl, combine the coffee granules, granulated sugar, and boiling water. Stir once to dissolve the granules and sugar. Using a handheld mixer, whip for about 4 minutes, until stiff, glossy peaks form. Add 1 to 2 Tbsp to the top of each ramekin of chocolate mousse. Refrigerate until ready to serve.

To assemble: Add 3 pretzels to the top of each ramekin and serve.

FEBRUARY

Syrah/Shiraz

chapter 2

Get ready to warm up this winter with Syrah!

No need to get all hot and bothered when you see some of the price tags on French and California Syrah—you can find the juice under its other name, Shiraz (common in Australia), at most wine shops and some are a steal! For learning purposes, I suggest you keep both the more expensive French and California Syrahs in the mix this month. You may spend a little more on the Syrah than Shiraz, but you'll definitely notice the difference when sipping side by side.

Getting to Know Syrah/Shiraz

These two grapes are like identical twins separated at birth. They are exactly the same genetically, but the flavor ranges dramatically in the glass. What you taste all depends on where these grapes were born and who raised them from the vine to the barrel. The Rhône region of France, especially the Northern Rhône, is hailed for its awesome Syrah, though there are a few gems to be found further south, like those in the Languedoc region.

Shiraz is by far Australia's darling little grape. The Aussies' ability to showcase how delish this grape can be has brought their wine industry fame and fortune. California calls it Syrah. South Africa calls it Shiraz. So, for this chapter when we talk about France and California, we'll call it Syrah, and we'll call it Shiraz when we talk about it being from anywhere else. You'll see the differences between the two once you start sniffing and sipping.

Rhône 101

All the wines you'll be tasting this month are clearly labeled "Syrah" or "Shiraz," except for the Frenchies. Because, as you know by now, the French generally name their wines after where the grapes grow instead of by the name of the grapes.

In general, wines from the Rhône region are called Côtes du Rhône. The Rhône region is split into two major growing areas, north and south, and it's the north we're after this month. While other grapes are grown in the Northern Rhône (namely the white grape Viognier, which you'll savor in chapter 5), the inky black Syrah grape dominates the area, labeled under the following wine-growing regions.

HERMITAGE AND CÔTE-RÔTIE These wines are considered the big kids on the block—they have big oak characteristics from the barrels they're stored in for aging, which translates to big tannins and high alcohol content. As you learned when drinking Cabs, these attributes make for a wine that's better after a few years in the bottle. You can uncork these when they are first released, but you'll miss out on the rich chocolate and tobacco characteristics that really come forward with age.

CORNAS, ST-JOSEPH, AND CROZES-HERMITAGE These are the next in line for popularity. (Less popular means more affordable, and that's right up my alley.) These babies are full of flavor and at a much more appealing price. Compared to the others, Syrah from St-Joseph or Crozes-Hermitage will be the most drinkable upon release.

SOUTHERN RHÔNE VALLEY If we dip a little farther into the Southern Rhône Valley, we'll find highly renowned wines made from the Grenache grape as well as some terrific wines made from various blends of grapes. The best known of the blends is Châteauneuf-du-Pape, a sexy red wine made from blending Syrah with many different red and white grape varietals—a total of thirteen different grapes can be used.

Blending red and white grapes? You bet! This happens more often than you think. In fact, while those Syrahs you're tasting from the Northern Rhône Valley are made mostly from the Syrah grape, most are blended with small amounts of white grapes; Viogner makes its way into the Côte-Rôtie, and small amounts of Roussanne and Marsanne (both yummy white grapes) can be found in the Hermitage, Crozes-Hermitage, and St-Joseph. Only the Cornas doesn't get a little white grape treatment—it's completely Syrah.

Stop right there—don't go memorizing the amounts of white wine that go into these Rhône Syrahs. The important thing is to remember that these Frenchies get a little something extra from some white grape varietals. Let's call it that certain *je ne sais quoi.*

It's All in the Smell

Wine doesn't always smell like roses, and Rhône Syrah can be one of those wines that brings a little funk to the table. If at first sniff you think you smell something offensive, don't keep it a secret: Discuss it with your fellow tasters. It is much harder to detect bad wine qualities in red wine than in white wine. That's because a lot of red wine aromas mask the flaws. However, there are certain foul aromas that are deemed acceptable. In future chapters, don't be surprised to see cat pee and barnyard as suitable sniffs in certain wines. For now, let's call them *acquired* aromas. I bet you never thought burning rubber would be an aroma you'd want in your wine, but for Syrah . . . oh, you'll see.

When it comes to Syrah, you'll smell everything from dark berries and plum-like fruity aromas to more than a dash of spice. However, before we get to swirling and sniffing all those nice things, let's talk a little bit about some of the smells that aren't so nice.

Cork Taint

You may have heard the term *cork taint* or *corked* used to describe a wine. It does not mean that the cork broke and some of it ended up in the wine, but that a faulty cork has allowed some TCA (a stinky chemical compound that comes from corks or the barrels where wine was aged or stored) to contaminate your wine. TCA isn't going to kill you—but it's a killjoy to wine.

Most of the time, TCA is present in such small amounts that it goes unnoticed. But sometimes the wine will exude a musty, moldy smell (it reminds me of my brother's dirty sweat socks, or the way our damp clothes smell the day after we play in the snow). When you smell that, don't drink the wine. If you're in a restaurant, send it back; if you bought the bottle at a wine shop, ask for a refund. And take note: An alarming number of bottles of wine are corked—between 5 and

15 percent, depending on whom you ask—so if you think your wine smells like sweaty socks, trust your judgment and open another bottle.

Cooked Wine

Another bad thing that happens to good wine is when it gets "cooked." The term means just what it says; somehow, after the wine was put in the bottle, it got too hot and sort of baked a bit. The result is a thin wine without any oomph, with aromas that are more like stewed prunes than fresh fruit. And while a stewed prune aroma is acceptable in certain wines like ports, it is not what you should smell in Shiraz—or most reds, for that matter.

Chances are, you've likely tasted a cooked wine without even realizing it. If you remove the capsule (the metallic covering on the neck and mouth of the bottle) and the cork shows signs of leakage or the neck of the bottle gives you sticky fingers, then the wine inside has most likely been cooked. Also, if you notice even before removing the capsule that the cork is poking through the foil, the wine has probably hit some high temps. Check out the cork in your bottle before you buy it—the cork should be snug as a bug in the bottleneck, and not poking out at all.

When it comes to cooked wine, there can be many culprits. Sometimes, distributors leave cases sitting outside in the heat; other times, stores don't have a proper cooling system in the summer months; even a hot delivery truck will do it. Or you may be the one to blame! I can't tell you how many times I've walked into friends' homes and have found they store their wine on top of the refrigerator. Do not do this! Usually, your fridge is warm on top, or warm air blows from the motor in the back—not a good thing for wine. If you don't have a wine cellar, a wine fridge, or a dry basement, keep your wine in the back of a closet or cupboard that is cool and dark. Your bottles can stay put there just fine for a while.

Sulfur or Burning Rubber

Stick your schnoz in a glass of wine, inhale deeply, and take in those aromas of fruits and spices and fresh cracked black pepper and . . . burning rubber?

What you're smelling isn't a tire plant, it's sulfur dioxide. This is commonly used in the bottling process to help preserve wine; however, when your wine is given an overdose of the stuff, it will be more pungent. Count this as one of those not-so-good aromas.

That is, unless you're drinking Syrah from the Northern Rhône. Then, believe it or not, that sulfur smell isn't actually from the addition of sulfur dioxide. Syrah that hasn't fully ripened can emit this burnt rubber smell. And certain parts of the Rhône region, like the Ardèche, are more likely to produce grapes that carry this smell. Some say this is actually a desired trait of the juice (leave it to the French). Usually, you can swirl the glass and the aroma blows off after a minute or two. Remember this nugget when you are swirling and sniffing. If you find a hint of this aroma, you can bet it's a Rhône Syrah.

Wine Speak

FRUIT-FORWARD This term is used to describe wines that show their fruit first before any other aromas or flavors. If at first whiff you get earth and spice, that wine is not fruit-forward. It's when you inhale and, depending on the wine, you are hit with berries or tropical fruits at first sniff. The same goes for your first sip: It should be fruit you taste first to use this descriptor for wine.

PETITE SIRAH Although the name sounds like Syrah, and the wine can look like Syrah, smell like Syrah, and taste like Syrah, it is not Syrah. This is an entirely different grape that is known to grow well in Northern California.

VIN DE PAYS French country wine that comes from a particular geographic region and is made from certain grapes. It is superior to vin de table because of the specificity of its production.

VIN DE TABLE French table wine that can come from anywhere in France and be produced from any grapes.

IT'S GOT LEGS

In the wine world, we often talk about a wine's "legs." To check out your wine's legs, swirl the wine in a glass. Notice those little streams of wine that form as the wine begins to trail back into the bulb of the glass? These are the legs.

When the streams are thin, a wine is said to have loose or thin legs, an indicator that the wine is light- to medium-bodied—Sauvignon Blanc generally has thin legs. Thicker legs signal a high alcohol content and can also indicate viscous, fuller-bodied wines like Cabernet and Syrah.

So, swirl that Syrah and check out those legs. Its body will be revealed to you before you ever take a sip.

February's Picks

This month we will taste Syrah from two regions of France, one from California, and an Australian Shiraz.

Rhône Region, France   ($15 to $20)

Côtes du Rhône, Côte-Rôtie, St-Joseph, or Crozes-Hermitage all hail from Northern Rhône, are full-bodied, and have seen some oak.

Languedoc Region, France   ($12 to $15)

About 80 percent of France's vin de pays (country wine) comes from the Languedoc region, nestled in the sun-filled South of France. Though it's known for quantity, the region also offers quality red blends that are round and jammy with hints of licorice, ginger, and spice. In general, these pours are more affordable and easy drinking than the nuanced wines of the Northern Rhône.

California   ($15 to $20)

The full-bodied Syrah from California shows its signature spice in the nose with black pepper, licorice, eucalyptus, and mint.

Shiraz from Australia   ($15 to $20)

This New World wine will be rich and intense with all those standard Syrah attributes of red fruit and spice, but with a bolder expression.

Ringer: Cabernet Sauvignon from California   ($15 to $20)

Last month, you imbibed Napa Valley Cab. So this month, let's jog your memory by including one as the ringer.

Get Your Drink On

Syrah and Shiraz show off differently once poured, but either way, you may be entranced by their red-purple velvet appearance. And more than any other grape, these wines emit an enormous variety of aromas. Some will deliver fruit first, while others will whop you with black pepper and spicy notes. Sometimes there are flowers and chocolate too. With so much going on in the glass, it may be hard to choose a favorite!

TIME AND TEMP

Syrah is a big, tannic red wine, and these are best enjoyed at room temperature. That means you shouldn't put it in your fridge (too cold) or on top of your fridge (too hot). Of course, room temperature varies whether you're in a castle or in a hut, but for a reference point, when talking wine, room temperature is usually around 62°F to 65°F [16.7°C to 18.3°C].

COLOR Syrah and Shiraz have darker purple hues than the Cabs you tasted last month. Their color can vary from brownish red to a deep, dark bloodred; the one with the brownish tinge is most likely the one from the Rhône. Syrah/Shiraz tends to have a denser, inky color. If there's one in the bunch that seems a little lighter in hue, you may be looking at the ringer.

AROMA The spice most often attributed to Syrah/Shiraz is fresh cracked black pepper. If you have a pepper mill, crack some pepper right before the tasting starts, and put a little ramekin out for your guests to sniff as they taste—it will help them perceive this aroma in the wines. You'll note that all Syrah/Shiraz tends to have black pepper and spice in the nose. The Rhône wines will be rich with raisin, spice, and smoky aromas, and you might detect chocolate, tobacco, leather, and earthy aromas too. While the Rhône wines may also exhibit plum and berry aromas, they're not generally as fruit-forward as the Aussie Shiraz, which tends to show ripe fruit aromas first, after which comes the layers of chocolate, black pepper, and sweeter spices. The California Syrah will also exhibit sweeter spices, like clove, and can bear floral aromas like violet. Continue swirling your Syrah/Shiraz, and you may also notice dark chocolate, cocoa, mint, and licorice. And if that's not enough, this grape can also display aromas of smoked meats and wet rocks! Your ringer will show black cherries, cassis, asparagus, bell pepper, and even vanilla.

TASTE Syrah tastes like it smells. You'll get spice and earth and raisiny ripe fruits along with ripe berries. Shiraz is a fruity red with pepper and chocolate notes. You will see more concentrated fruity character up front with Shiraz. Rhône Syrah is a little shyer about expressing big bold fruit, but it is definitely there right alongside the spice.

BODY Syrah/Shiraz tops the list for full-bodied wines. It's lush on the palate, with full tannins that usually linger, and it has a very rich mouthfeel. You'll note that the ringer this month will have big tannins, but the mouthfeel may not be as silky and rich.

FINISH These big reds are often high in tannins, and if you get a very young Rhône Syrah, it can leave your mouth puckery. It's not that they're sour; rather, it's the dryness of the tannins that draws your cheeks together. Well-made Syrah/Shiraz is a harmonious balance between fruit and tannins in the finish.

FEBRUARY

Recipes

Syrah/Shiraz

LET'S EAT This spicy red wine pairs well with winter comfort foods and is even great when you get grilling. It also works well with pizza, of all things. Now that's my kind of wine! People often think you have to serve rich and creamy French food with red wine. While that may work in some cases, I find that simple foods pair just as well.

A little heat, a little sweet, and a nice crunch make these a perfect bite to go along with your glass of Syrah. You can make these in advance and freeze or refrigerate a couple of days before serving. Just be sure to warm them up for wine club.

Spicy Sausage, Sweet Potato, and Quinoa Bites

MAKES 20 TO 22 BITES

1 cup [140 g] cubed peeled sweet potato

³/₄ cup [140 g] cooked quinoa

8 oz [230 g] spicy breakfast sausage, casing removed

³/₄ tsp salt

1 egg

Honey mustard, garlic aioli, or ranch dressing, for dipping

Preheat the oven to 350°F [180°C]. Line a baking sheet with foil.

In a microwave-safe bowl with ½ in [13 mm] of water, add the sweet potatoes and cover with plastic wrap. Microwave on high for 6 to 7 minutes, stirring once halfway through. Remove and drain off the excess liquid. Use a fork to mash completely. Cool to room temperature.

In a large bowl, stir together the quinoa, breakfast sausage, smashed sweet potato, salt, and egg until evenly combined.

Roll the mixture into 1½ in [4 cm] meatballs. Place onto the prepared baking sheet and bake for 20 minutes. Then place under the broiler for 2 minutes to get a nice golden-brown color.

Let sit for 10 minutes before serving with the dressing for dipping. These can be made a couple of days in advance and stored in the refrigerator. Reheat in the oven for 10 minutes or until warm before serving.

French Bread–Burrata Pizza with Arugula

This beats frozen French bread pizza by a mile. Tomato butter is a great trick for using up any leftover tomato paste—it's super flavorful and toasts beautifully. And when you break open a ball of burrata and spread the creamy cheese on top—well, that's a treat in itself.

MAKES 24 PIECES

French Bread Pizza

1 baguette, split in half lengthwise (as if for a sandwich)

2 Tbsp olive oil

1 Tbsp garlic powder

2 Tbsp grated Parmesan cheese

1/2 to 3/4 cup [40 to 60 g] shredded mozzarella

Two 8 oz [230 g] balls burrata

Extra-virgin olive oil, for drizzling

1/2 cup [10 g] arugula

Kosher salt

Red pepper flakes (optional)

Position a rack in the center of the oven and preheat the broiler to high. Line a baking sheet with parchment paper.

To make the pizza: Place the baguette cut-sides up on the prepared baking sheet. Brush the cut sides of each with the olive oil, then sprinkle evenly with the garlic powder and the Parmesan cheese. Place the baking sheet on the middle rack and broil for 2 minutes, or until toasted and golden brown. Remove from the oven.

Reduce the oven temperature to 450°F [230°C].

To make the tomato butter: In a small food processor, add the butter, tomato paste, and garlic. Pulse until evenly combined. Spread the tomato butter evenly on the toasted baguette.

To finish the pizza: Sprinkle the shredded mozzarella evenly over both halves. Place the baking sheet pan back into the oven and bake for 5 to 6 minutes, until bubbly.

Tomato Butter

½ cup [110 g] unsalted butter, at room temperature

3 Tbsp tomato paste

1 Tbsp minced garlic

Using your hands, break apart the burrata and spread one ball on each baguette half. Drizzle with extra-virgin olive oil and sprinkle with the arugula, salt, and red pepper flakes (if desired) to finish.

Slice each half of the baguette into 12 pieces and serve.

This is a nutty take on the beloved sweet and savory Devils on Horseback hors d'oeuvre.

MAKES 24 PIECES

12 dates, cut in half and pitted

2 oz [55 g] goat cheese

24 whole blanched almonds

6 thin slices prosciutto, each cut into 4 strips

2 to 3 Tbsp olive oil

Dates with Goat Cheese, Almonds, and Prosciutto

Fill each of the halved dates with ½ tsp of goat cheese. Push one almond down into the center of the goat cheese. Wrap one strip of prosciutto around each stuffed date.

In a sauté pan over medium-high heat, heat the olive oil and cook each wrapped date on all sides for about a minute per side, until the prosciutto is crispy and a bit caramelized. Remove from the pan and drain on a rack or paper towels. Serve warm or at room temperature.

It's amazing what you can make from what's in your pantry. This dessert takes less than 10 minutes to assemble and it's fun to make. One bite of the salty, sweet, nutty bars is a perfect end to this month's wine club.

Salty Sweet Toffee Bars

MAKES 16 SQUARES

2 cups [200 g] Cheddar Goldfish crackers

3 cups [600 g] potato chips

One 8 oz [230 g] package Heath toffee bits

¼ cup [30 g] chopped pecans

One 14 oz [400 g] can sweetened condensed milk

Preheat the oven to 350°F [180°C]. Line an 8 by 8 in [20 by 20 cm] baking dish with parchment paper.

Place the crackers and chips into a gallon-size [3.6 L] zip-top bag. Using a rolling pin or wine bottle, crush up the crackers and chips until some coarse chunks remain (not into fine crumbs).

Place the smashed crackers and chip mixture into a bowl with the toffee bits and pecans. Toss to combine evenly. Add the condensed milk and stir to evenly coat.

Press the mixture evenly into the prepared pan and bake until the mixture is set, 20 to 25 minutes.

Remove and cool completely in the pan. When cool, use the parchment to remove the bars from the pan, cut into 16 squares, and serve.

Chardonnay

Now that spring is on the horizon, we're switching gears from red wine to white.

Put on your drinking shoes: We're kicking up our heels with the queen of whites, Chardonnay.

I'm no weather girl, but I can predict that when the wind turns warm, whites are far more fun than big reds. Chardonnay is the perfect start for our foray into whites because it is the most popular white wine grape in the world.

Let's face it, Chardonnay (we'll call it "Chard" for short) has gotten a pretty bad rap. A few years back, the American palate decided the bigger, more buttery, and oakier the Chardonnay, the better. So that's exactly what winemakers gave us. Overly oaky wine is no fun to sip and doesn't play well with food. Chard's other misperception is that it's basic. You'll see it's nothing of the sort.

This month you'll learn about another side of Chardonnay—the side that keeps thousands and thousands of wine lovers continually coming back for more. You'll see that this grape ranges dramatically in style, because I'm taking you well beyond the realm of those overly oaked pours and into a world where exquisite Chardonnays thrive.

Getting to Know Chardonnay

Around the world, Chardonnay is blended with Pinot Noir and Pinot Meunier for Champagne and bubbly wine, and it is the starlet of those yummy blanc de blancs bubblies you will taste test in December. If that's not enough to make you love it, Chard is also one of the noble grape varieties that can stand alone without being blended. Because the grape is relatively easy to grow, it is a favorite of vineyard managers worldwide.

Today, you can order a glass of Chard almost anywhere, but in the 1960s, it was relatively unknown outside of France. Can you imagine? Now it grows in Australia, California (Carneros and the southern Central Coast are cool regions where delish Chard can be found), Oregon, Argentina, South Africa, Washington State . . . well, Chard vines are practically everywhere, because the grape is so adaptable, unlike other whites such as Riesling and Sauvignon Blanc.

Burgundy Brings It On

We've all been baffled by French wine labels, because generally they don't tell you what grape was used to make the wine. But if the juice is from Burgundy, you can bet on the grape just by knowing whether the wine is red or white: If it's red it's Pinot Noir, and if it's white it's Chardonnay. These two grapes thrive here, and the Chardonnay from Burgundy is delish!

There are a number of subregions in Burgundy, but when it comes to Chardonnay, these are the ones to remember.

CHABLIS Do not confuse this for a bulk wine. Although in the United States this name was slapped on many a jug to make a sale, this is in fact a phenomenal French wine-growing region. Chablis is the northernmost region of Burgundy, close to Champagne. Here, many of the Chards are aged in stainless steel rather than oak, so the flavors are cleaner, with a crisp acidity and minerality; they typically smell of gunflint (this will be that smell you can't identify off the top of your head—at least probably not!).

CÔTE-D'OR This region is where the majority of Burgundy's great wines come from and is considered Chardonnay's true home—some say its spiritual dwelling. Côte-d'Or literally means "golden slope," and the Chard coming from this soil is definitely worth its weight in gold. The Côte-d'Or comprises two sections: the Côte de Nuits—mostly known for its reds—and, further south, the Côte de Beaune, which also produces reds but is especially celebrated for its whites. Within the region, the winemakers have such different techniques that their wines are quite diverse; pinning a defined style on this region is nearly impossible. Puligny-Montrachet, Chassagne-Montrachet, and Meursault are villages in the Côte-d'Or that are especially renowned for their whites.

CHALONNAISE AND CÔTE MÂCONNAIS These two regions make great Chard at much lower price points. While the everyday drinking wines are considered the plain Janes of white Burgundies, they still maintain the characters of the grape and they're awesome served cool on a warm day.

The Many Flavors of Chard

BUTTERY This is a li'l wine science, but don't worry, it's easy to digest. The buttery taste in many Chardonnays comes from a wine-making process called malolactic fermentation, where crisp, tart acids are converted into softer acid (think green apple versus the acid found in milk). The process produces a compound that reduces the acidity and makes the wine rounder, creamier, and what we call buttery in character. Wines like Riesling and Sauvignon Blanc most likely won't undergo malolactic fermentation, as acid is a quality that winemakers strive to keep in those particular white wines.

OAKY Wood and wine sounds like a gross combo, but barrel-aging Chardonnay lends flavors and deeper golden colors that make this wine unique. Most everywhere, Chardonnay is fermented (that's when the juice turns into alcohol) and aged (that's when the wine then gets to rest and round out) in oak barrels. When playing with oak, the winemaker really determines the fate of the resulting wine. If the wine is left too long in oak, it will taste like, well, oak and not fruit. When done well, the oak will impart a fuller body and flavors of vanilla, butter, and toasted nuts without masking the fruit. In some big operations, winemakers will take the easy route and impart that oaky flavor by using oak chips. You should not be hit in the face with the taste of oak. It should be a part of the wine's character, not the defining characteristic, as is often the case.

Most often, American Chard is aged in oak (you know, those wine barrels you see geeky winemakers leaning on while holding a glass of wine for their cover shot?). Some of the most popular types of oak used in these barrels are Hungarian, American, and French oak. Each oak lends its own attribute to the juice. For example, American oak is known for the vanilla flavor it imparts, and Hungarian oak can lend a note of spice to the finished wine. These oak attributes can completely change the taste and mouthfeel of any grape's juice.

You may often hear that a wine is aged in "new oak." That means that the wine will have stronger oak characteristics, whereas Chard aged in used oak barrels will show the subtleties of the wood. The best Côte-d'Or producers barrel ferment the juice, using at least a percentage of new oak and aiming to achieve just the right balance of the wood and the wine. How much oak mingles with your wine is completely up to the winemaker, but in general you'll find more oak in California Chard than you will in any of those from France.

How can you tell whether it's oaked? California Chardonnay usually says right on the back label whether or not it's hit with oak, so turn it around and give the back label a once-over before buying. If the label doesn't specify whether the wine has been aged in steel or oak, just ask someone working at the wine shop. (Don't be shy; when you're at the grocery store and you can't find the peanut butter, you ask for it, right?)

Wine Speak

GRAND CRU A wine that's considered better than premier cru. In Burgundy, this designation is given to the thirty-four top wineries. It literally means "great growth" and translates to "open your wallet wider." These are best eight to ten years after bottling.

MÂCON-VILLAGES A popular wine from the Mâconnais region of Burgundy. These are almost always made without oak, giving you a crisp, delish sip for about $15 per bottle.

POUILLY-FUISSÉ The most famous of the wines from the Mâconnais region of Burgundy, and the fullest-bodied. Made from Chardonnay grapes, these wines are usually aged in oak, taste best when young, and are priced starting around $20 per bottle.

PREMIER CRU "First growth." Without getting too technical, this refers to Burgundy wines that are considered superior to wines with "villages" designations (such as Mâcon-Villages). These beauties shine five years after they've been bottled but can hang out in the cellar for up to ten.

March's Picks

This month we'll taste Chard from California, Argentina, Australia, and two places in France. By sipping Chards from cooler regions alongside Chards from hot spots, you'll get to taste the effect of climate on this grape.

California   ($15 to $30)

The color of these Chards will range from shades of yellow to gold. If they are oaked, they will have darker colors and oaky aromas of vanilla and butter. Flavors of green apple, lemon, and orange are typical, as are nutty, buttery, and spicy tastes that come from the oak aging.

Argentina   ($10 to $14)

These Chards will be close to California Chardonnay in looks, aroma, and taste. They may also bring some white peach and honey notes.

Australia   ($10 to $12)

These New World Chards will have more tropical fruit aromas and flavors like pineapple, mango, and banana.

Côte Chalonnaise or Mâconnais, France   ($15 to $30)

The climate here is a bit warmer than the Côte-d'Or, so these chards will show riper fruit characteristics like white peach and apple along with honeysuckle and citrus peel. You will get some terroir or earthiness from all the French Chard this month.

Premier Cru from the Côte-d'Or, France   ($30 to $45)

These subtle Chards will be lighter in color, aroma, and taste than those from the New World regions. Burgundy whites show clean flavors of apple and pear up front but will also have mineral characteristics like wet rock aromas.

Ringer: Pinot Grigio   ($10 to $15)

For this tasting, throw a Pinot Grigio into the mix. Pinot Grigio is a very easy-drinking, light-bodied white wine. It will typically be lighter in color, have more citrus fruit aromas, and have a much shorter finish than the Chards in the tasting.

THE VANILLA EFFECT

A very common flavor and aroma in Chardonnay is vanilla, a component that comes from the oak barrels in which the wine was aged. When you taste it, you can be sure you're sipping a Chard that hooked up with oak at some point previous to your pour. Here is a great exercise to help you learn whether you prefer oak or not. First, pour two half-glasses of oak-free Chardonnay. Take a vanilla bean and scrape the seeds into one of the glasses. (If you can't find a vanilla bean, you can use $\frac{1}{2}$ tsp of vanilla extract.) Sniff the two glasses side by side: Do you prefer the vanilla aromatics? Or do you think it covers the fruity nose? Now taste them side by side. Does that vanilla complement the wine? Or do you prefer the cleaner version sans vanilla? If you like it fruitier smelling and cleaner tasting, stick to buying white Burgundies. However, if you find that vanilla yummy, go for California Chards.

Get Your Drink On

This is a really fun tasting, as without a doubt you have some pre-conceived notions of this famous wine. However, when you taste them side by side, you may be shocked which whites you favor. Celebrating Chardonnay this month may or may not turn you into a loyal fan of this great grape, but there's only one way to find out, so get sipping!

TIME AND TEMP

Like most wines from the New World, Chardonnay is made to drink young, except for the premier and grand crus of Burgundy, so don't hold on to them for too long.

No matter when you pull the cork, Chardonnay should not be served too cold. Oaked Chards definitely taste even more oaky when served too chilly. If you pull the bottles from your fridge at least 15 minutes before pouring, you'll be in good shape.

You can drink Chard any time of the year, depending on the style of the wine. But because it is high in alcohol and often low in acid, it's best to avoid on a scorching hot day. Overall, a steely clean Chard from Chablis best suits the warmer months, and rich and buttery Chards from California make for good sipping all winter long.

COLOR In general, the Chard from Burgundy will be lighter, more straw-colored than those from California. The Aussie Chards lean toward being darker gold in color. If the color is darker, the body will be richer—two sure signs you are not sipping Chardonnay from Burgundy, France. Aged Chards can have a brownish tinge, but since we're not tasting a vintage Chard this month, if yours looks brown it's more likely to be a telltale sign that the wine is bad.

AROMA The Burgundies will show the grape characteristics first, with apples and pears in the nose, along with their earthy character, with mineral and wet rock aromas. The oaked California Chard will show its oak first, but it is also very fruity with citrus, green apple, and peach. California Chard is famous for that buttery aroma. There are a couple of California Chardonnays that don't have any oak, though, so don't be so hasty to guess the origin. Aussie Chard smells more like tropical fruits, such as pineapple, banana, and mango.

TASTE Overall, Chard from Burgundy will be the most subtle of all the styles. California Chard will taste like the fruits you smell—lemon, orange, and green apple—along with that vanilla and butter. The Chard from Down Under will show riper fruit flavors, like pineapple and mango you smell. Chardonnay aged in oak barrels can taste buttery, nutty, and spicy. As you taste, see whether you can detect the difference climate makes: Does one taste like green apple (typical of cooler climates) and the other like pineapple and tropical fruits (typical of warmer climates)?

BODY Burgundy Chards are lighter in body and refreshing, with a crisp and more acidic style than those from the New World. California Chards are the richest and heaviest whites we'll taste.

FINISH In general, the New World Chardonnays are bigger all the way around. So, it follows suit that their finish is bolder and lengthier than that of the Frenchies.

MARCH

Recipes

Chardonnay

LET'S EAT Pairing Chardonnay with food can be tricky. If the wine is too oaky, then it will take over the food. Clean and acidic Chablis is a great complement to plain seafood (oysters, in particular), however, if the seafood is served swimming in a butter sauce, or beurre blanc, a full-bodied and buttery Chardonnay would be the best companion. But for now, these bites are playful pairings for both styles of Chardonnay. Grab some napkins and find your faves.

Everyone loves tater tots.
Serve them with
this simple spicy mayo
and you've got a home
run bar snack.

1 lb [455 g] frozen tater
tots

$\frac{1}{4}$ cup [20 g] grated
Parmesan cheese

$\frac{1}{2}$ cup [120 g] mayonnaise

2 tsp sriracha (or your
favorite hot sauce)

Tater Tots with Spicy Mayo

Bake the tater tots according to the package
instructions. Halfway through baking, turn the
tots over and sprinkle with the grated Parmesan. Place back in the oven for the second half
of cooking.

In a small bowl, stir the mayonnaise and the
sriracha until evenly combined.

Serve the cooked tots on a plate or platter with
the spicy mayonnaise in a small bowl or ramekin for dipping.

MAKES 24 PIECES

2 Tbsp olive oil

2 cups [320 g] corn kernels cut from the cob

One 15 oz [430 g] can chickpeas, drained and rinsed

1 small red bell pepper, finely diced (about $3/4$ cup [90 g])

2 green onions, thinly sliced

$1/2$ cup [20 g] chopped fresh cilantro

1 large jalapeño, seeded and finely diced

$1/4$ cup [60 ml] fresh lime juice

3 Tbsp sour cream

2 Tbsp mayonnaise

$1/2$ tsp ground cumin

$1/2$ tsp chipotle chile powder

$1/2$ tsp paprika

$3/4$ cup [90 g] crumbled cotija cheese (you can substitute feta)

Coarsely ground salt

24 endive leaves (about 3 heads)

This bright, fresh appetizer is a spin on the traditional Mexican street corn salad, incorporating chickpeas for a more substantial bite. Alongside Chardonnay, it's a star.

Chickpea Street Salad

In a large cast-iron skillet over high heat, heat the olive oil. Once hot, add the corn and cook for 2 to 3 minutes to brown.

In a large mixing bowl, combine the chickpeas, bell pepper, green onions, cilantro, jalapeño, and corn. The corn mixture can be made ahead of time and refrigerated.

In a separate small bowl, combine the lime juice, sour cream, mayonnaise, cumin, chipotle chile powder, and paprika until evenly mixed. Add this to the corn and chickpea mixture and toss to evenly coat. Add the cotija cheese and stir to combine. Taste and season with salt if needed.

Spoon generously into the endive leaves and serve immediately.

Who knows why smoked salmon always takes the spotlight? Smoked trout is the winner in my book. Chardonnay in new oak barrels often has a smoky aroma, and this appetizer can stand up to it. You'll make more pickled red onions than you'll need but you'll be happy to have them in the fridge when your next salad or sandwich needs a pick-me-up.

Smoked Trout Pâté on Baguette with Quick Pickled Red Onions

MAKES 24 PIECES

To make the pickled red onions: Add the onion to a pint jar with a tight-fitting lid, packing it in firmly.

In a small saucepan over medium heat, heat the vinegar, ¼ cup [60 ml] water, the honey, and peppercorns just until the honey is dissolved. Add the hot mixture to the jar slowly until the onions are completely covered. Set aside. These onions can be used after an hour or kept in the fridge for up to a month.

To make the trout pâté: In a bowl, stir together the trout, sour cream, mayonnaise, chopped dill, lemon juice, and horseradish until evenly combined.

Quick Pickled Red Onions

1 medium red onion, very thinly sliced

¹/₂ cup [120 ml] apple cider vinegar

1¹/₂ Tbsp honey

¹/₄ tsp black peppercorns

Trout Pâté

8 oz [230 g] smoked trout, skinned and flaked

¼ cup plus 1 Tbsp [75 g] sour cream

¼ cup plus 1 Tbsp [75 g] mayonnaise

¼ cup [10 g] chopped fresh dill

3 Tbsp fresh lemon juice

1 Tbsp horseradish

To assemble

24 baguette slices

3 dill sprigs, picked, for garnish

To assemble: Place the baguette slices on a platter and top each with the trout pâté. Top each with a spoonful of pickled red onions. Add a tiny sprig of fresh dill on top of each. Serve immediately.

Three simple ingredients make for a pretty, and pretty delicious, bite. Using presliced Cheddar makes for even quicker assembly, but you can buy a block and slice your own too. The key here is the Spanish-style dry-cured chorizo. Be sure not to buy soft or fresh Mexican-style chorizo—you want the hard link, like salami, for slicing.

Chorizo, Apple, and Cheddar Bites

On a plate or platter, arrange 16 to 18 squares of cheddar. Shingle 2 thin slices of apple on top of each slice of cheese. Place one thin slice of chorizo on top of the apples. Secure together with a toothpick.

MAKES 16 TO 18 BITES

One 10 oz [280 g] package sliced sharp yellow Cheddar cheese (you'll only use half the package)

1 large (or 2 small) Granny Smith apples, thinly sliced (32 to 36 slices)

1 link dried Spanish-style dry-cured chorizo, cut on the bias into sixteen to eighteen 1/8 in [3 mm] thick pieces

If you've never tried really good extra-virgin olive oil drizzled on ice cream, you're in for a treat. Sprinkle a little flaky sea salt and it's a dessert epiphany. These are best when the waffles are freshly toasted, cooled but still crispy, then assembled to serve.

MAKES 12 ICE CREAM SANDWICHES

1 pint [480 g] vanilla ice cream, slightly thawed

24 store-bought mini waffles (can be found in the freezer section), toasted and cooled

Extra-virgin olive oil

Flaky sea salt, such as Maldon

Mini Waffle Ice Cream Sandwiches

Use a melon baller to place one scoop of ice cream on half of the waffles. Place another waffle on top.

Drizzle with olive oil and sprinkle with the sea salt. Serve immediately.

You can make the ice cream sandwiches and freeze ahead of time—just drizzle with oil and sprinkle with salt just before serving.

APRIL

Merlot &
Other Reds

chapter 4

This month we'll skip around the globe tasting some softer reds like Merlot and learn about some heavy hitters like Barolo. You could spend your life getting to know all the red wines out there, but we'll focus on a few well-known pours and clink a couple of fun new reds too.

April is an in-between time with chilly evenings that can call for a red, or warm sunny days that merit a glass of white. Lighter reds, including Merlot (*mur-LOW*), are perfectly suited for this transition. It's normal to crave big reds when it's chilly and acidic whites when it's sweltering hot out. Because this month is just warming up, you'll meet a bunch more reds that fit the bill for both. Though Merlot is not the only red suited for the season, it is the one we'll spend the most time learning about.

Getting to Know Red Wine

Merlot may be the only wine that has gotten so far on its texture and body alone. For this reason, lots of wine snobs see it as a simple wine that lacks complexity and character. But Merlot continually wins the popularity contest for its approachability and availability. It blends well with other grapes, like Cab and Cab Franc, and it pairs well with plenty of foods. Merlot is shyer than Cab, but that doesn't make it any less of a wine. Jancis Robinson, a famed wine authority and Master of Wine, describes Merlot as "Cabernet without the pain." Wine club is all about less pain and more pleasure, so let's get to it.

The Bordeaux region's most planted black grape is Merlot. It's part and parcel of France's great wines from the Saint-Émilion and Pomerol regions. Both of these spots produce Merlot-based wines; however, staying true to the style of Bordeaux, they're not made from just the Merlot grape. Just like Cabs from Bordeaux are not straight-up Cabs, these Merlot-based wines are also blended, mostly with Cabernet Sauvignon. Merlot is thinner-skinned than Cab, which means its juice is lighter in color and lacks that kick-you-in-the-teeth acidity; it also doesn't come with those austere tannins like Cabs do.

Although Cab often gets more credit from wine drinkers than Merlot, Merlot is a much better-behaved grape in the vineyard and the glass. In the vineyard, the grape ripens before Cab and more often has a successful growing season; in the glass, it brings smoothness that Cab can only achieve when blended or when aged. Merlot vines pretty much grow all over the world, including France, Italy, Switzerland, Slovenia, Hungary, Romania, Bulgaria, Russia, California, Washington State, New York, Argentina, Chile, Australia, New Zealand, and South Africa. Widely available translates to affordable, and pleasing price tags mean you can try many Merlots without going broke.

A notable exception is Château Pétrus, a very famous wine from the Pomerol district of the Bordeaux region. Made with 95 percent

Merlot, it costs close to $1,000 a bottle upon release; older vintages can get upwards of $5,000 at auction!

Cabernet's Right-Hand Man

Cabernet and Merlot are very similar in flavor profiles. Where they differ is in intensity and body. Remember, Cab is a big wine—big flavor, big alcohol, big tannins. Merlot? Not so big. High alcohol provides viscosity, and we perceive this viscosity as the body. Most often Cabs are higher in alcohol than Merlot, and are thus fuller-bodied wines. Once again, this is the wine world we're talking about, so of course there are exceptions; for example, some more expensive Merlots from California and Washington State can be just as high in alcohol as Cabs, making them much bigger wines on your palate.

While Cab and Merlot differ, they are more alike than most want to admit. In France's famed Bordeaux wines, Cab brings on the big guns, but when Cab is blended with Merlot, you get a wine with balance and character. In California, winemakers replicate this art of blending in what's called Meritage-style wines (see Wine Speak on page 95). And the United States isn't the only player in the New World to make these Bordeaux-esque blends. Winemakers the world over blend Cab, Merlot, and other traditional Bordeaux grapes for their takes on Bordeaux-style wines.

Other Reds You Should Be Sipping

As mentioned, the number of red wines in the world is far too many to tackle at one wine club meeting. We've covered Cabs and Syrah so far this year, and now we're getting in deep with the beloved Merlot. But let's take a spin around the globe and get into some other attention-worthy reds.

Italy

LAMBRUSCO Italy is flush with fun, affordable red wine. First up, let's get fizzy with a li'l Lambrusco, the perfect gateway wine to summer. Lambrusco is a pretty red sparkling wine from the middle of northern Italy's Emilia-Romagna region. This happy wine ranges in color from rosé to red and from sweet to dry. Typically, it is light and served chilled or on ice. This month, look for one from the Reggiano region (yes, that sounds familiar because it's also where the famed cheese, Parmigiano-Reggiano, hails from). Look for these terms on the label:

- Secco: on the dry side
- Semi-secco: semidry, usually made in the frizzante style (see Wine Speak on page 95)
- Amabile: semisweet
- Dolce: all in on the sugar

BAROLO This big red comes from the northwest Italian region of Piedmont and is made with 100 percent Nebbiolo grapes. Tannins, acidity, alcohol, and flavor are all huge in the glass. Often called the king of reds, this wine has common aromas of tar and dried fruit. Note that all the hype comes with a hefty price tag.

CHIANTI Tuscany's darling red grape, Chianti is made from at least 75 percent Sangiovese grapes. In general, this juice is medium-bodied, with mild tannins, cherry-strawberry fruit, and earthy spice. It's a very dry red and typically acidic and tannic. Tart foods balance that tannic acidity, so you'll find it works with most food, especially Italian fare. When buying Chianti, look for the words *Chianti Classico*, which means the wine comes from the heartland of Italy's Chianti region. Chianti Classico Riserva signals the wine has been aged longer in oak barrels, lending more tannins and structure, along with aromas of smoke and spice. One of the best parts of this sip is that you can find yummy Chianti for around $10 per bottle.

BRUNELLO DI MONTALCINO Called "Brunello" for short, this big red is from Tuscany and similar to Barolo in strength. They are both heavy hitters, so no light sipping here. Some aromas you may find when swirling include cranberry, coffee, licorice or anise, and earthy notes. With great acidity and structure, this is a special red worthy of savoring.

BARBERA D'ASTI OR BARBERA D'ALBA From Piedmont, this grape makes for an easy-drinking, bright, light red perfect for spring. It's a fruity sip with strawberry, raspberry, cherry, and blackberry aromas and flavor. (Think fun wine, similar to French Beaujolais in style and depth.) Depending on where the grapes are grown, either in the town of Asti or Alba, you will see it named that on the label.

NERO D'AVOLA This Sicilian wine is full-bodied with dark fruit and nutty flavors. If you dig Zinfandel, this month reach for a Nero d'Avola instead.

Spain

RIOJA This classic Spanish wine is made mostly from the Tempranillo grape. Wines at the top end can taste full, rich, and velvety—a bit like a great Bordeaux—but less expensive Riojas have their charms too. Like Pinot Noir and Chianti, these lighter Riojas, with their bright berry flavors, are great spring and summer reds. You'll notice Rioja is classified in four ways:

- Rioja: The standard.

- Crianza: Usually aged in used oak. This is the lightest, fruitiest, least oaky, least expensive style—think good house red.
- Reserva: These are required to age at least three years, one of those being in oak, so they are heavier, and a little pricier.
- Gran Reserva: At the top of the heap is gran reserva, which spends at least two years in oak and three more in the bottle before you get to sip. That much oak makes these the heaviest, oakiest, and most costly, and they are made only with the best grapes in the best years.

CARMÉNÈRE   In recent years, it was discovered that vines in Spain that were thought to be Merlot were actually Carménère. This grape used to be common in Bordeaux but is no longer used for those blends. Merlot drinkers will especially like Carménère—it's dark, rich, and smooth, with nice plum flavors. Carménère also comes from Chile, so you may see that while wine shopping.

Argentina

MALBEC   The most notable red wine from this country comes from the Mendoza region. Malbec from Mendoza is rich with tannins and oak, dark in color, very juicy, and brings a little spice. It's like a Cabernet Sauvignon, but usually less expensive. Expect black fruits like plum, blackberry, and black cherry along with tobacco and leather. A fun red alternative to the typical Cabs.

Greece

XINOMAVRO   The Xinomavro (*ksee-NO-mav-roh*) grape, while not über-popular, is still super fun to taste. From Macedonia, these wines will be intense and raisiny, and might have a slightly medicinal tang. Their big tannins and acidity put them next to Barolo for style.

Wine Speak

BLACK GRAPES Grapes used to make red wines. Merlot, Cabernet Sauvignon, Syrah, Malbec, and Tempranillo are just some of the many black grapes.

EARTHY Describes wines with aromas and tastes reminiscent of wet rocks, minerals, or mushrooms.

FRIZZANTE This is an effervescent Italian wine style.

MERITAGE Wines made in the United States in the style of the great Bordeaux wines. The typical blend for reds most often includes Cabernet Sauvignon, Merlot, and Cabernet Franc, but may also include Petit Verdot and Malbec. There is also a white Meritage.

SPUMANTE Term used for Italian wines that have more fizz than frizzante.

OXIDIZED WINE

In March, we talked about how wine can taste gross if it's been corked, cooked, or wrought with too much sulfur. Oxidized wine is a wine that has been exposed to too much oxygen. This is different from the aeration we're aiming for when swirling a wine. Overexposure to oxygen can happen during the winemaking process; it can also be caused by a faulty cork or the wine being open too long, which happens frequently in restaurants that serve wine by the glass.

With white wines, you may be able to notice oxidization before you even take a sip. Oxidized whites turn amber and then brownish in color, just like a cut apple turns brown when exposed to oxygen. Reds don't show it so much in the color, but one sip and you'll know—oxidized wine is lifeless. You won't get a pleasant fruity aroma or a nice full body. The wine will be flat and fruitless, and in extreme cases, it tastes like vinegar.

If you want to learn about it firsthand, open a bottle of Merlot a week to ten days before your wine club. Pour yourself a glass and re-cork the bottle by gently pressing the cork back into the neck. Don't re-cork with a Vacu Vin or any other wine-saving device. Leave the bottle on the countertop until the tasting. On the day of, cover with foil and place this bottle into the mix with the other freshly opened wines. Taste them side by side with the other wines and you'll never forget what oxidized wine smells and tastes like.

April's Picks

Old World Merlot   ($30 to $60)

Choose one from France, either Pomerol or Saint-Émilion (you may find some between $20 and $30 a bottle, but most will be priced between $30 and $60 a bottle).

New World Merlot   ($12 to $18)

Try one from California or Washington State. This will probably be the biggest red wine of the bunch.

Lambrusco   ($15 to $20)

While the famed and widely available Riunite is sweet, branch out and seek a secco, or dry, version of this fizzy wine for the tasting. Remember to chill before serving.

Barbera d'Asti   ($15 to $20)

Head to the Italian section of your wine shop for this one. A Barbera d'Alba will also work for this tasting.

Malbec   ($12 to $20)

You may even find some under $15. If so, go for it!

Rioja   ($12 to $15)

Go for a Crianza, the lightest of the bunch from Rioja.

Get Your Drink On

Time for your red wine–tasting adventure. Most of the reds we'll taste this month will be fun, lighter-bodied pours. For learning purposes, our lineup includes two Merlots, one Old World, and one New World so you can taste side by side and see the difference a place can make to a grape. You'll also taste wine from Italy, Argentina, and Spain. As we mentioned, there are dozens and dozens of other reds out there, so if something else catches your eye while you're shopping, by all means, cover it in foil and slip it in this month's mix. This is *your* wine club, after all, and you can do it any way you like. Now gather your glassware, some good friends, and get to sipping.

TIME AND TEMP

This month, we'll follow Merlot's lead for time and tasting advice. All of these light reds are meant to be enjoyed young, meaning there's no need to store or cellar them for a later date. If they are on the shelves of your wine shop, they are ready to pour now.

Keep these reds a little cooler than your average home temperature. If you are hosting wine club al fresco this month, you can put the bottles in the fridge for 30 minutes before serving. Unlike the other reds in this chapter, your Lambrusco should be well chilled and you can even serve over ice if you'd like.

COLOR This month's wine will range from lighter ruby hues to inky red. The one with a little shimmer or bubbles will be a dead giveaway as Lambrusco. But can you find the Malbec with its customary purple tinge? Pay attention to whether the light shines through your pour or whether it is opaque. The darker the wine, the stronger the flavor and aromas. Here's another tip to remember: Red wine gets lighter as it ages and white wine gets darker.

AROMA See whether your wine shows fruit first or earthy mineral notes. New World is typically fruit-forward. With red wines, you'll sniff everything from juicy berries, like strawberries, blueberries, raspberries, and blackberries, to plummy, jammy, black cherry notes and on to watermelon, violets, roses, earth, iron, and mineral aromas. Riper fruits are a sign of the Old World style. If at first you only smell alcohol, take a step back, swirl a few times, and try again. Reds are higher in alcohol than whites, so you can get nasal fatigue faster. And most of these are young, so you may have to sniff and swirl a few times before you find something. Some other smells to expect include oak, cocoa or milk chocolate, sweet tobacco, vanilla, and sweet spices like clove and cinnamon.

TASTE This group of bottles was chosen to show off the softer side of red, but still with great fruits (like you'll be smelling in the previous aroma list) and terroir. Oak aging might show up as vanilla or spice when you sip, but again, it will be subtle.

BODY Merlot is famous for its soft, smooth, medium body. French Merlot will be lower in alcohol than a California Merlot. Therefore, the one from the United States will be bigger. The others in the bunch will range from light to medium body.

FINISH These will all have a shorter finish than the Cabs or Syrahs you sipped this year. Notice the softer tannins, and how your mouth isn't taken over by them. See whether you like it and want another sip.

APRIL

Recipes

Merlot &
Other Reds

LET'S EAT Reds range from big fruit-forward wines to softer, more sensitive sips, and pair with everything from grilled red meat to salty cheese. This month we have it all, so be sure to come hungry!

Blue Cheese, Roast Beef, and Grape Skewers

To make the horseradish mayonnaise: In a small bowl, add the mayonnaise, horseradish, lemon juice, and garlic powder, and mix until combined. Set aside.

To assemble the skewers: On a skewer or toothpick, skewer a piece of the roast beef like a ribbon, adding a dot of horseradish mayo in the middle of it, then add a cube of blue cheese, then a grape, flat side down so that they stand upright when placed on a plate or serving dish. Repeat with the remaining skewers.

Blue cheese with red wine is one of the best happy hour pairings. Add in tender roast beef, a touch of horseradish mayo, and a sweet, juicy grape, and you have the perfect bite. If you run out of time to thread these three ingredients onto toothpicks, you can simply serve them on a plate or platter with a small dish of the horseradish mayo on the side and toothpicks for picking them up.

MAKES 24 SKEWERS

Horseradish Mayonnaise

$\frac{1}{2}$ **cup mayonnaise**

2 Tbsp prepared horseradish

1 tsp fresh lemon juice

$\frac{1}{2}$ **tsp garlic powder**

Skewers

4 oz [115 g] thinly sliced rare roast beef, cut into quarters

Blue cheese, cubed

24 seedless green or red grapes, with one end of each trimmed off to create a flat side

The perfect appetizer is one that you can pop right in your mouth while holding your wineglass at the same time. These deep-fried olives are just that. Who knew an olive could be so good? These are stuffed with mozzarella, but you can use provolone too.

Deep-Fried Green Olives

**MAKES ABOUT
40 OLIVES**

4 cups [960 ml] canola oil

2 eggs beaten with 2 tsp water

1 cup [140 g] Italian seasoned bread crumbs

2 oz [55 g] mozzarella cheese, cut into 1 by $\frac{1}{4}$ in [2.5 cm by 6 mm] pieces

One 8.5 oz [240 g] jar large pitted green olives

In a deep fryer or heavy-bottom pot, heat the oil to 375°F [190°C] on a deep-fry thermometer. Pour the egg wash into a shallow bowl and spread the bread crumbs on a shallow plate.

Place one piece of cheese snugly into each olive. Dip the stuffed olive in the egg wash and then roll it in the bread crumbs. Work in batches of 10 olives.

Using a slotted spoon, carefully place the olives into the hot oil. Cook for 30 to 45 seconds, until golden brown. Remove and place on a paper towel–lined plate to drain.

Resist the temptation to pop one in your mouth until they have cooled for at least 5 minutes. Allow the oil to reheat (unless you have a deep fryer that can maintain a constant temperature) between batches. Cool for at least 10 minutes before serving. These are best served warm but can be served at room temperature as well. Do not refrigerate after frying.

French Onion Crostini

Preheat the oven to 425°F [220°C]. Line a baking sheet with parchment paper.

In a large cast-iron skillet or heavy-bottom pot over high heat, melt 2 Tbsp of the butter. Once foamy, add the sliced onions and toss to coat. Lower the heat to medium. Cook, stirring occasionally, until the onions are deep golden brown and soft, 20 to 25 minutes, being careful not to burn them. Add the red wine and scrape up any brown bits from the skillet with a wooden spoon. Cook for 2 minutes. Add the chicken broth and cook for 3 to 5 more minutes, until the liquid has evaporated. Remove from the heat and season with ¼ tsp of the salt and freshly ground black pepper.

This rich, umami bite covered in gooey melted Gruyère is inspired by the very first thing I made at the Culinary Institute of America: French onion soup. You can and should caramelize the onions and toast your crostini ahead of time to make for super easy assembly on the night of wine club. Simply store your toasted baguettes in an airtight container and reheat your caramelized onions before assembly.

MAKES 12 CROSTINI

4 Tbsp [55 g] unsalted butter

2 large onions, sliced (4 cups [640 g])

¼ cup [60 ml] red wine

½ cup [120 ml] chicken broth

½ tsp coarsely ground salt

Freshly ground black pepper

12 slices baguette

1 garlic clove, cut in half

¾ to 1 cup [60 to 80 g] grated Gruyère cheese

3 Tbsp finely chopped fresh chives

In a small microwave-safe cup or bowl, melt the remaining 2 Tbsp of butter in the microwave. Place the baguette slices in a single layer on the prepared baking sheet. Brush with the melted butter and sprinkle with the remaining ¼ tsp of salt. Bake for 8 to 10 minutes, until golden brown and toasted. Remove from the oven and let cool for 5 minutes (keep the oven on). Rub the garlic clove over the top of each crostini (if making ahead, you can store the crostini in an airtight container until ready to serve). Reheat the onion mixture, if needed, and top each crostini with 1 Tbsp of the onion mixture, then generously top each with the Gruyère. Bake for 3 to 4 minutes, or until the cheese is melted, bubbly, and golden brown. Remove from the oven and sprinkle with the chives.

You'll totally get why these are addictive as soon as you taste them. In fact, I promise you'll love them so much that you'll add them to your regular wine club repertoire, red wine or not.

Simply Addictive Sugar and Spiced Nuts

SERVES 12 TO 14

1/3 cup [65 g] dark brown sugar

2/3 cup [130 g] white granulated sugar

1 1/2 tsp kosher salt

1 tsp ground cinnamon

1 tsp roughly chopped fresh rosemary

1/4 tsp cayenne pepper

1 egg white

1 lb [455 g] walnuts, pecan halves, or almonds (or a combination)

1/2 cup [60 g] pine nuts

Preheat the oven to 300°F [150°C]. Line a baking sheet with parchment paper.

In a small bowl, combine the sugars, salt, cinnamon, rosemary, and cayenne.

In a separate bowl that's large enough to hold all of the nuts, beat the egg white with 2 tsp of water with a fork until frothy.

Add the nuts to the egg white and stir to coat evenly. Sprinkle the nuts with the sugar mixture and toss until evenly coated.

Spread the sugared nuts in a single layer on the prepared baking sheet and bake for 20 to 25 minutes, stirring occasionally, until brown and toasted through. Remove from the oven, and separate the nuts as they cool. Serve at room temperature.

The almighty JC—Julia Child—created a perfect clafouti that most cooks use as their standard, including me. Here I made them individual, added almond extract, and used cherries to complement our red wines.

MAKES 12 INDIVIDUAL CLAFOUTIS

1¼ cups [300 ml] whole milk

3 eggs

⅓ cup [65 g] granulated sugar

2 tsp almond extract

¼ tsp salt

⅔ cup [90 g] all-purpose flour

2 cups [280 g] frozen sweet cherries, pitted

Confectioners' sugar, for serving

Individual Cherry Almond Clafoutis

Preheat the oven to 350°F [180°C]. Spray a 12-cup muffin tin with baking spray.

In a mixing bowl, whisk together the milk, eggs, granulated sugar, almond extract, and salt until smooth and frothy. Add the flour and whisk until evenly incorporated.

Add 2 Tbsp of the mixture to each muffin cup. Evenly distribute the cherries among the cups and top with the remaining mixture to cover the cherries. Each cup will be filled to the top.

Bake for 30 to 35 minutes, until the clafoutis are set and a skewer inserted into the center comes out clean.

Let cool for 10 minutes before transferring the clafoutis from the muffin tin to a cooling rack. Serve warm or store in an airtight container until ready to serve. Place the clafoutis on a tray and sift confectioners' sugar over the top before serving.

Viognier & Other Whites

This month, we're switching it up from focusing on one single grape to include a whole bunch of white wines for you to taste. If you're bored ordering the house white wine, or picking up the same Chardonnay every Friday just doesn't jazz you anymore, this wine club is made for you. Contrary to their name, white wine grapes are not white: Those grape bunches are greenish, maybe dark yellow, and can be pink too, and they all lend different flavors to your glass. There are hundreds of white wines out there and you could spend years tasting them. So this month, get ready to trek around the globe to try lesser-known white wines from France and Italy and hop over to Portugal and Greece for some sipping too. Some of these whites you may be familiar with, such as Pinot Grigio, and others may be completely new to you. Either way, after May wine club, you'll know wherein lies your favorite white wine.

Getting to Know White Wine

We're going to spend a chunk of time this month on a little white grape called Viognier (*vee-oh-NYAY*). Side by side, Viognier and Chardonnay look like they could be sisters. They also share traits of low acid and full alcohol, but the similarities stop there. With one sniff, it's undeniable that Viognier is far sexier than Chardonnay. It's famous for being floral. There is fruit there, too, but the fun part of this pour is finding bouquets of gardenias, honeysuckle, and orange blossoms in your glass.

Like Chardonnay, Viognier comes from both the Old World—France's Northern Rhône Valley, to be specific—and the New World. The most notable difference is the fuller fruit and more in-your-face florals of the New World versus the more subdued, nuanced pours from the Old World. Floral Viognier from either area makes for a fab aperitif (predinner drink), is great as a spritzer enjoyed alfresco with friends, and is perfect for a picnic in the park with your honey.

Georges Vernay, famed winemaker in Condrieu, France (the spot where world-class Viognier hails from), believed in this fickle grape. The vines of Condrieu are believed to be some of the oldest, if not *the* oldest, in France, and they grow on steep and rocky terraces. Growing and harvesting these grapes is the real definition of backbreaking labor, and Vernay was there for it. The results produce gorgeous, musky Viognier with hints of apricot, peach, and exotic fruits.

The Rhône's other most famous white wine–growing region is Château-Grillet, also famous for this grape. While most Viognier should be drunk young, winemakers and experts alike say you can age Château-Grillet for up to twenty years.

We mentioned in February that this white grape is blended with Syrah to produce the red wine Côte-Rôtie. It is very rare for the French to allow a white grape to mingle with the likes of such a highly esteemed grape as Syrah. But in Côte-Rôtie, the addition of Viognier delicately softens the Syrah and adds depth to its aromatics. This just goes to show that this white wine is worthy of your attention.

Wood in White Wine

All white wine, Viognier included, is mainly fermented and/or aged in stainless steel, plastic, glass, cement, or oak barrels. Why do we care? Well, this part of the winemaking process makes a huge difference in what we end up drinking. Of the options, the oak is the big player, bringing color, texture, aromas, and flavors to the glass.

New oak, which means a freshly made and toasted barrel, imparts the boldest aromas, flavor, and texture. It turns a clear wine to richer hues of straw and even gold and shows up as vanilla, caramel, coconut, toast, and warm baking spices like cinnamon and clove as you sniff, swirl, and sip. New barrels also add tannins and structure. As barrels are used and reused, the barrels become more neutral and impart softer notes.

American oak is bolder and known for that butter and vanilla, whereas French oak lends nutty and smoky elements to the wine. In either case, barrels breathe, and that air helps round out or add weight to a white wine, creating creamy and fuller-bodied sips than those aged in stainless steel. Stainless steel tanks are airtight, so no additional flavors or aromatics end up in the wine, letting the true essence of the grape shine bright.

During your wine club tasting this month, pay attention: Is your white wine golden-hued with notes of toast and vanilla, or would you describe it as clear, crisp, and refreshing? Your answer will tip you off to how your wine was made. Look at that. It's only been four months of wine club and you're basically a winemaker now!

Other Whites You Should Be Sipping

Grab your glasses. It's time to meet some more great whites. The list below is just a sampling of the many white wines you should try. It spans the world from France to Greece and Italy, which is, in particular, serving up several very sippable, not to mention affordable, whites perfect for wine club.

First Up, France

MARSANNE AND ROUSSANNE From the Northern Rhône Valley come these two famous white wine grapes. Both are used to mix with Syrah in parts of the Rhône to soften out those huge reds. But on their own, they're quite interesting. Marsanne makes deep-colored white wines that are fairly full-bodied and sometimes described as waxy. The best of the bunch have a citrus perfume and notes of almond paste, with concentrated orange marmalade and peach flavors. Acid's not this wine's strong point, so Marsanne is best drunk young. Roussanne is often blended with Marsanne. You can find bottles that are straight-up Roussanne, but it's less likely. These wines can smell like herbal tea and, like Marsanne, have flavors of lemon with a slip of earthiness and that slightly unusual waxy texture. The yummy ones taste like fresh pears and honey. Remember, French labels can be tricky—Marsanne and Roussanne wines from the Rhône are not labeled by the grape, but by the appellation: Look for a white wine from Crozes-Hermitage, Hermitage, and St-Joseph. Unless you know that a specific producer is making their white with all Marsanne or all Roussanne, if you get a white from one of these spots, you're most likely sipping Marsanne with a splash of Roussanne.

MUSCADET Not to be confused with the Muscat grape that makes the sweeter Moscato, this is a crisp, tart, dry number with apple, mineral, and occasionally a wave of grapefruit. Helpfully, major French Muscadets have the word *Muscadet* in their titles—in this case, the appellation includes the name of the grape; examples include Muscadet, Muscadet Sèvre-et-Maine, and Muscadet Coteaux de la Loire. Merci.

Next Stop: Germany and Austria

GRÜNER VELTLINER Austria's most famous white wine is known as Grüner for short. Think citrus, citrus, and more citrus. Sometimes, bell pepper shows up here and this wine can be spicy. An adjacent sip to Sauvignon Blanc, Grüner is perfect for summer cookouts and easy on the wallet.

MÜLLER-THURGAU You'll taste delish German Rieslings in June, so this month you may want to give another German white wine, Müller-Thurgau, a go. Müller-Thurgau is the most commonly grown grape in Germany, producing semidry, light wine. You could also pick up a bottle of this guy from Oregon or Washington for this month's shindig.

Over to Italy

PINOT GRIGIO (NORTHERN ITALY; ALSO CALLED "PINOT GRIS" IN FRANCE) In recent years this grape has made its way into everyday wine vernacular. If you have yet to try it, you're in for a fun, approachable quaff. PG is crisp, dry, and light- to medium-bodied. Some can be nondescript—watery, even—but typically you'll get great fruit like apples, pear, peach, and citrus aromas and flavors. This is a perfect all-occasion wine, especially for weddings. Its personality is easy to get along with and it loves lots of different foods, especially appetizers.

GAVI (PIEDMONT) This pour is named for the Gavi wine-growing region in Piedmont, not the grape. The wine is a dry, acidic white made from the Cortese grape, and has a straw color and a neutral, mild aroma. Gavi di Gavi (meaning Gavi from Gavi) is the ultimate. If you're a Sauvignon Blanc diehard, branch out: I promise you will add this to your list of faves, and it makes for a lovely clink before a big Italian dinner.

VERNACCIA DI SAN GIMIGNANO (TUSCANY) Love, love, love this little white. There are various white grape varieties called Vernaccia that grow throughout Italy; the word is related to "vernacular," implying a local or native vine. Vernaccia of San Gimignano, however, is what you want. It's grown nowhere else but around the town of San Gimignano in Tuscany. Often blended with a splash of Chardonnay, these wines have a distinctive almond and spice flavor that is light and easy drinking.

VERMENTINO DI GALLURA (SARDINIA) Vermentino is a tough grape that grows in adverse conditions on the island of Sardinia. Its hallmark feature is its herbaceous aromas (think mint, sage, oregano, etc.), which it picks up from other plants grown in the area. If you don't do fruity whites, this wine is for you.

Last Stops: Spain, Portugal, and Greece

ALBARIÑO (ALVARINHO IN PORTUGUESE) One of Spain's and Portugal's most prized white wine grapes. The Portuguese use it to make blends for Vinho Verde. It's medium- to full-bodied and makes your mouth water with citrus fruits, flowers, and peach, and is sometimes stitched with minerally, wet stone flavors and a touch of salt or brininess. Next time you order the seafood tower, get a bottle of this to go with it.

VINHO VERDE Go to Portugal. Seriously, if you're planning a European vacay, this is where you should go to sip light spritzy white wines, like Vinho Verde. *Verde* means "green," and the term doesn't describe its color, but the fact that you're supposed to drink it young. These

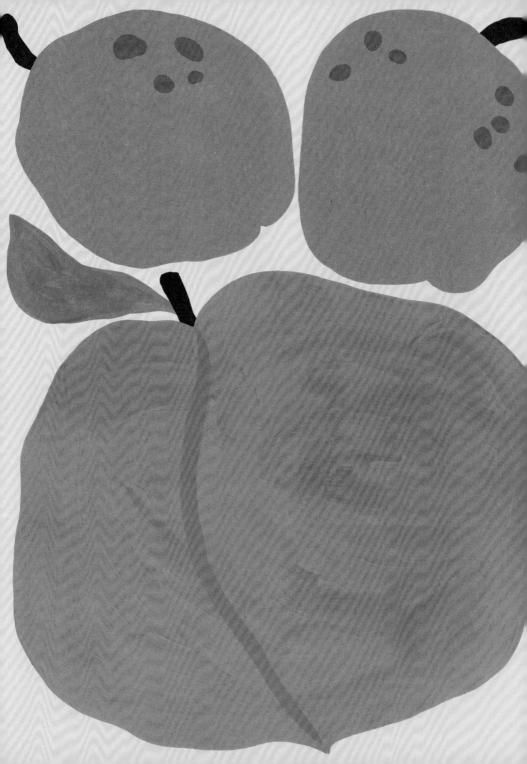

whites make for great sipping on warm, even hot, days. They're crisp with lemony flavors and a hint of fizz and are usually lower in alcohol, making for a great lunch wine.

ASSYRTIKO Although Greece practically invented wine, these days they're merely considered an "emerging wine region"—probably because people think of the wretched Retsina (in short, it's Greek white wine that's mixed with pine resin). But respectable pours come from the mainland as well as the Greek islands. When going Greek, throw on a bathing suit and have a vacay with this light, minerally, acidic, dry white wine from Santorini.

Wine Speak

APERITIF An alcoholic beverage enjoyed before eating to stimulate the appetite. A white wine spitzer using Viognier is an awesome aperitif.

AROMATIC Refers to a wine that has an intense aroma that's true to the varietal.

BRIGHT Describes the look of a clear wine; also used to describe the flavors of fresh, clean wine.

FLORAL Describes wines that smell more like a flower shop than a berry patch or a pile of dirt. Most commonly, you'll notice roses, gardenias, violets, and orange blossoms when sniffing floral wines.

RICH Describes a full mouthfeel, full aroma, or intense flavors.

SUR LIE This is a term you may see on the back of a wine label. It indicates a wine was aged on its lees (the solids that settle to the bottom), which lends structure and a little body to the wine as well as a signature yeasty aroma and often a spritz.

May's Picks

Choosing this month's lineup was like choosing a favorite child; there are so many white wines to love. However, the winners represent an array of interesting and unique varietals that hopefully show you white wine in a new light.

Viognier ($15 to $20)

Viognier from Condrieu starts at about $45 per bottle, whereas those from Château-Grillet are priced closer to $65 and up. Viognier wines from the Languedoc region are less expensive and easier to find. You can also taste this grape from California, Chile, or Australia for a fraction of the cost of the Frenchies.

Marsanne, France ($15 to $20)

Include one from the Hermitage region for the best example of this grape.

Pinot Grigio, Italy ($15 to $20)

The standard is Santa Margherita, which showcases a fabulous Pinot Grigio, but it will ring in a little pricier than other PGs.

Grüner Veltliner (Under $20)

Look for one under 12.5 percent ABV to get that acidic mouthwatering experience.

Albariño (Under $20)

An Albariño from Spain's Rias Baixas region or a Vinho Verde from Portugal (or both) are perfect for wine club this month.

SCREW THE CORK

The screw cap—you've seen it, now let's talk about it. Old-school wine lovers hate the idea of not pulling the cork. But the fact of the matter is that screw caps have been proven to preserve the integrity of wine far longer than corks. I won't get into the science of it, but corks let air in and screw caps don't. These days, savvy wine-makers have caught on to that fact, so you can no longer assume that every wine with a screw cap is of lesser value. Great wines as well as crappy wines are now being packaged with screw tops. One South African winemaker politely told me to "screw the cork" when I asked how he felt about the ongoing cork debate. There you have it: World-class wines can and do wear this shiny hat. As long as what's in the bottle is worth it, I don't care how you give it to me.

And just so you know, it takes twenty-five years for a cork tree to bear useful cork. After that, the tree can only be stripped every nine years. Whether you have an environmentally conscious bone in your body or not, logically you can see why this may not be the best bet for bottling wine.

Get Your Drink On

This tasting brings all the white wine things to the table. From highly acidic wine that feels like it's stripping the enamel from your teeth to rich and round pours with a touch of oak, your white wine prowess is about to skyrocket. Our variety of white wines this month will showcase a range in each of the following categories, but use what's here for reference. Happy sipping!

TIME AND TEMP

Chilled white wine can benefit from being warmed to room temperature. As with all wine, a bottle that's overly chilled will "lock up" the aromas and flavors, holding them hostage until it warms up to temperature. Traditionally, wines are served at "cellar temperature," that is, about 55°F [12.8°C]. But because we're against sticking thermometers in our wine, just make sure the wine is chilled enough to be refreshing, but warm enough for you to detect those great aromas and flavors. If wine is too cold, go ahead and take the bowl of the glass in your hands and swirl it around; the heat from your hands will warm the glass, and in turn, the wine. While this might not be "the" appropriate thing to do (according to wine snobs who might insist you have a proper temperature-controlled wine storage unit), who cares? You're with friends, after all.

A side note here: If you do prefer your wine ice-cold, more power to you—tasting wine is all about personal preference. But try letting it warm up a touch one time and see what you think.

COLOR Clear to golden, pale straw to deeper yellow colors. No matter where the juice comes from, when you look at it, it should be bright, not dull.

AROMA All the fruits: apple, pear, apricot, peach, lemon, lime, grapefruit, tropical fruit like pineapple, passion fruit, and mango. All the flowers: honeysuckle, gardenia, and orange blossoms. Sweet spices like cinnamon and clove; and you might find earthiness, musky, minerality, wet stones, briny notes, and elements from oak (think toast, vanilla, and coconut).

TASTE From sweet to dry and fruity to austere. The tastes may be similar to the aromas above. Just note whether it tastes pleasing to you and whether it's good enough for you to go back for more.

BODY White wines will range from light- to full-bodied. If it shows tannins at all, they are soft tannins, and you'll notice them on the insides of your cheeks. Most will be lighter-bodied, but if it feels round and rich in your mouth, it is fuller-bodied.

FINISH Note the acidity of the wine. Is your mouth watering? The finish may feel stringent or it may have finesse. A well-made white will have good acidity, leaving a fresh and vibrant finish that lingers just long enough for you to crave another sip.

MAY

Recipes

*Viognier &
Other Whites*

LET'S EAT This month's simple and spicy menu is inspired by the many flavors of the Mediterranean. Because our wines are so varied, it makes sense that the food pairings follow suit. But if you are pressed for time, you can put out a mezze spread of store-bought hummus, tzatziki, baba ghanoush, fresh chopped veggies (such as bell peppers, cherry tomatoes, and sliced cucumbers), pickled veggies, olives, and an assortment of crackers and pita bread.

How well does your wine handle a little heat? Find out with this creamy and spicy hummus alongside a chilled glass of white.

MAKES 2 CUPS [480 G]

One 14 oz [400 g] can chickpeas, drained

1/4 cup [60 ml] fresh lemon juice (from about 2 lemons)

1/4 cup [60 ml] ice-cold water

2 Tbsp tahini

1 Tbsp red curry paste

1 tsp garlic powder

1/2 tsp kosher salt

1/4 cup plus 2 Tbsp [90 ml] olive oil

Pita chips, for serving

Super Spicy Hummus

In a food processor or blender, add the chickpeas, lemon juice, water, tahini, curry paste, garlic powder, and salt and pulse briefly to combine. With the motor running, drizzle in the olive oil and purée until smooth. Transfer to bowl and serve with pita chips.

Keeping a box of puff pastry in your freezer is a pro entertaining trick. In just minutes, this unassuming sheet of dough can be turned into a variety of appetizers, like these crispy, garlicky cheese straws that love a good glass of white.

Garlicky Parsley and Parmesan Cheese Straws

MAKES 20 STRAWS

One 17.3 oz [490 g] box puff pastry (2 sheets), thawed

1 egg beaten with 1 tsp water

2 garlic cloves, minced

1/4 cup [10 g] chopped fresh flat-leaf parsley

1/2 cup [50 g] grated Parmesan cheese

Preheat the oven to 400°F [200°C]. Line a baking sheet with parchment paper.

Dust your work space lightly with flour. Open your puff pastry sheets, place them side by side on your work surface, and pinch them together to form a single large sheet. Brush the dough with the egg wash and sprinkle the garlic, parsley, and 1/4 cup [25 g] of the cheese evenly over the top.

Using a pizza wheel, cut the dough into twenty strips about 1 in [2.5 cm] wide. Don't worry if they seem too skinny; they will puff up. Twist the ends of each strip in opposite directions and place them onto the prepared baking sheet. Brush the dough again with the egg wash and sprinkle with the remaining 1/4 cup [25 g] of cheese.

Bake for 12 minutes, or until golden brown and puffy.

These are best the day they are made, but you can make them a day in advance, cool, and store in an airtight container.

Pop one of these in your mouth and you'll feel like you're in Greece or Turkey. This recipe calls for a lamb and beef mixture, but you can also make the meatballs all lamb or all beef if you prefer. These really shine when you dip them in the lemony yogurt sauce and get a bit of the preserved lemon peel all in one bite.

Mediterranean Meatballs with Greek Yogurt and Preserved Lemon Peels

Preheat the oven to 400°F [200°C]. Line a baking sheet with parchment paper.

In a large bowl, stir together the beef, lamb, eggs, bread crumbs, oregano, cumin, ginger, and salt until evenly mixed. Roll into 1½ to 2 in [4 to 5 cm] meatballs—they should be big enough for one or two bites max. Place onto the prepared baking sheet. Bake for 20 minutes, then place under the broiler for 2 minutes more to get them nice and golden brown.

Serve the meatballs on a platter with the lemon peels sprinkled on top and a small bowl of the yogurt sauce alongside.

MAKES 25 TO 30 BITE-SIZE MEATBALLS

12 oz [340 g] lean ground beef

12 oz [340 g] ground lamb

2 large eggs, lightly beaten

½ cup [70 g] seasoned bread crumbs

1 Tbsp dried oregano

1 Tbsp ground cumin

1 Tbsp grated peeled fresh ginger

2 tsp salt

Easy Preserved Lemon Peels (recipe follows)

Yogurt Dipping Sauce (recipe follows)

2 lemons, preferably organic

1 Tbsp fresh lemon juice

1 Tbsp sugar

1 tsp salt

$1/_4$ tsp red pepper flakes

Easy Preserved Lemon Peels

Using a vegetable peeler, cut strips off of the lemons, being careful to avoid the pith, then cut each strip crosswise into three pieces. In a small bowl, combine the lemon peel pieces, lemon juice, sugar, salt, and red pepper flakes and let sit for at least an hour. These can be made up to 1 week in advance and stored in the fridge until ready to serve.

1 cup [240 g] plain Greek-style yogurt

3 Tbsp extra-virgin olive oil

2 Tbsp fresh lemon juice

1 tsp grated lemon zest, plus more for garnish

$1/_4$ cup [10 g] chopped fresh flat-leaf parsley, plus more for garnish

Kosher salt and freshly ground black pepper

Yogurt Dipping Sauce

In a bowl, stir together the yogurt, oil, lemon juice, lemon zest, and parsley until combined. Taste and season with salt and pepper. Garnish with more lemon zest and a sprinkle of parsley.

This is the cutest salad you will ever eat. It is also one of the most refreshing and delicious. With all its awesome fresh veggies and tangy feta cheese, it is the ideal partner for a lovely white wine this month.

Mini Greek Salad Bites

MAKES 12 TO 14 BITES

Line a baking sheet with paper towels. Using a melon baller, scoop out the cucumber pieces, leaving a solid layer of flesh on the bottom, to create a cup. Place the cucumber cups scooped-side down on the paper towels to absorb moisture.

To make the dressing: In a small jar with a tight-fitting lid, add all of the dressing ingredients and shake until emulsified.

To make the salad: In a bowl, combine the red bell pepper, cherry tomatoes, feta, olives, and mint. Add 1 Tbsp of the dressing and toss to evenly coat, then add more dressing if desired.

To assemble: Fill the cucumber cups with the salad. Transfer the salad bites to a serving dish.

1 English cucumber, peeled and cut into $^3/_4$ in [2 cm] pieces

Dressing

2 Tbsp extra-virgin olive oil

1 Tbsp red wine vinegar

$^1/_2$ tsp dried oregano

$^1/_2$ tsp garlic powder

$^1/_4$ tsp Dijon mustard

$^1/_4$ tsp salt

Salad

$^1/_4$ cup [30 g] finely diced red bell pepper

$^1/_4$ cup [40 g] finely chopped cherry tomatoes

2 Tbsp crumbled feta cheese

2 Tbsp finely chopped black or Kalamata olives

2 tsp chopped fresh mint

Store-bought madeleines, little French sponge cakes shaped like shells, are so delicate and pretty. Split them and fill with this peach ice cream hack, and now they're a perfect sweet ending for this month's wine club. Be sure to make enough that each guest can have two.

Peach Marmalade Ice Cream Gems

MAKES 20 PIECES

1 pint [480 g] vanilla ice cream

3 Tbsp peach marmalade

20 store-bought madeleines, halved lengthwise with a serrated knife

Remove the ice cream from the freezer and place the container on the counter for 10 minutes.

In a large bowl, place the ice cream and work it with a wooden spoon or spatula until it is soft. Be sure not to work the ice cream too much— it should look like soft-serve ice cream, not soup. Fold in the marmalade.

Place the ice cream back into its container and place in the freezer until completely frozen again, about 1 hour. (This will make more ice cream than needed for this recipe. Enjoy the leftovers on their own or alongside another dessert!)

Put a plate in the freezer. When the peach ice cream is frozen again, place 1 Tbsp of it on each madeleine bottom and top with the other half of the cookie. Place the assembled mini ice cream sandwiches onto the plate in the freezer a couple at a time so they do not melt. These can be made a week in advance and removed from the freezer just before serving.

JUNE

Riesling

chapter 6

When it comes to frolicking in the sun, my go-to wine used to be bubbly or rosé. However, a recent unofficial backyard taste test of picnic foods alongside the all-time summer favorites—sparkling wine, rosé, and Pinot Grigio—and newcomer Riesling showed Riesling emerge as the champ. From sandwiches and salads to pâté and pickles, it went so well with everything. You'll see Riesling works well in summer because it's relatively low in alcohol (as low as 8 percent), which makes it a great wine to drink when you're hanging outside on a sunny day. But after the picnic trials and further food and wine taste testing, this lovely little white has made its way into my spring and fall lineups as well.

This month, go ahead and move your wine club outdoors. Spread a patchwork of picnic blankets under a tree or settle onto the front porch or backyard deck. You're about to discover why fresh, bright, and breezy June is the month to fall in love with this whimsical wine.

Getting to Know Riesling

The Riesling grape is often misunderstood. Somewhere along the line, Americans got the idea that Riesling was unsophisticated and sugary sweet—a training-wheel wine on the level of wine coolers or white Zinfandel.

America's opinion of this pour is still suffering slightly from the collective hangover that the sweet German Riesling wine imported back in the 1970s and '80s wrought. It was incredibly popular then, but it took a hit when American wine drinkers started to get more serious about wine and move away from super-sweet sips. The assumption was that all Riesling was as saccharine sweet as Blue Nun, a popular wine at the time, or as boring as the worst kinds of other Liebfraumilch (German Riesling-based wines).

Even these days, you've probably heard someone say, "Well, I just don't like sweet wines," when offered a Riesling. Their loss! Not all Rieslings are sweet. In fact, they can range from sweet to quite dry; plus, there's nothing wrong with sweetness in your wine—the best Rieslings balance their sweetness with a piercing acidity. It's a clean kind of sweetness that's not cloying in your mouth. The combo of pure fruit flavor zipped up with a crisp zing can be a beautiful thing indeed.

The charms of Riesling are slowly being rediscovered by Americans, but a lot of people still don't quite get it. That's good for us, because until Rieslings become wildly popular, they'll remain a good value; there are still some awesome finds to be had for around $10 to $15 a bottle.

The Cool Beauty

Don't go hunting for Rieslings in Spain, Italy, or the South of France; the finest Rieslings are produced from grapes grown in colder climates, as the grape needs to ripen through a long, cool season and hang on the vines until autumn. While it's true you'll find Rieslings in Australia and California, these will be much more full-bodied, without that racy acidity you'll taste in wines from grapes grown in cooler climates like northern Germany and Alsace. When looking for Riesling, reach for those from these relatively northern regions of wine-growing countries.

MOSEL-SAAR-RUWER Located in the north of Germany, this is one of the country's finest wine-growing regions. Riesling dominates the super-steep slopes here, and it's where the grape truly shines—the wines from this area are exquisite and nuanced, with a touch of sweetness. For your tasting, a bottle of wine from this region is a must so that you can see just how elegant this grape can be.

ALSACE, FRANCE While other grapes are grown here, Riesling is the grape of Alsace—the most prestigious and widely planted in the region. Remember how for Chardonnay you had to look for the Burgundy region if you wanted to find one from France? Alsatian wines are much easier to decode, because Alsace is the only wine-growing area in France where wines are named by grape, not region. If the wine inside is made from the Riesling grape, it's called Riesling right on the bottle. Doesn't that make life easy? Although Alsace is right next door to Germany (and, in fact, used to be part of Germany), the Rieslings from this area are completely different from those from the Mosel-Saar-Ruwer. Alsatian Rieslings are known for their amazing acid and fruit balance and their steely, mineral-like characteristics. Well-made Rieslings from this area become more refined as they age; in fact, when they're young, they're somewhat closed up, so in general, I look for bottles that are at least three years old. If you want to drink them young, reach for the least expensive bottle you can find, because they are usually the lightest in style and more ready to drink. Long-necked, slender green bottles are used to package Alsatian Riesling, in particular, and indicate a dry wine. This style of bottle has also been used

for Riesling from other parts of the world. So, in a blind tasting if you see an elongated bottle hiding under wraps, you should be tipped off that you will be tasting Riesling or another style of Alsatian or German wine like Gewürztraminer.

NORTHERN AUSTRIA Again, although Austria and Germany are neighbors, their Rieslings are nothing alike. Austrian Rieslings are more full-bodied, powerful, and fruit-forward than German Rieslings; they're often described as vibrant and lively, smelling of rose and peach. They may be difficult to find, so they're not required for your tasting this month.

FINGER LAKES, NEW YORK Riesling is a major grape grown in New York State, and the styles here range from dry to off-dry and the über-sweet late harvest and ice wines. For me, the best Rieslings in the United States come from this region—it's well worth seeking one out for your tasting. If you're headed to the Big Apple or already sweltering in the city, a weekend road trip to this region is also super fun and delicious.

While these are the most renowned regions for Riesling, the grape is also grown and produced in Washington State, Oregon, California, Australia, New Zealand, South Africa, and Canada. To be honest, some are awesome, some aren't. When starting out, the safest bet is to focus mostly on Rieslings from the regions detailed above. That way, you can taste the best and decide for yourself later on whether you like the rest.

Wine Speak

A.O.C. (APELLATION D'ORIGINE CONTRÔLÉE) This is a term you may see on a bottle label this month. It's a formal designation, conferred by the French government for wines grown and produced in the region of their origin using traditional processes. Other countries have similar systems.

AUSLESE, BEERENAUSLESE, EISWEIN, TROCKENBEERENAUSLESE These categories of German wines are straight-up sweet, and are listed here from sweet to sweetest.

HALBTROCKEN/SPÄTLESE Think "kinda dry/kinda sweet." *Halbtrocken* is German for "half-dry" and refers to a wine that's a little bit sweeter than Trocken wines. *Spätlese* refers to a particular category of wine that's also half-dry—or slightly sweet.

LIEBFRAUMILCH This style of German white wine is too sweet for many. But even if the one you choose is one-dimensionally sweet and boring, tasting it will help you understand why German wines got such a bad rap.

RACY A term often used for that pleasing zippy quality that comes from the acidity in white wines.

TROCKEN, CLASSIC, SELECTION, KABINETT These terms all indicate "dry." *Trocken* literally means "dry" in German; the other terms are various designations found on labels of German wines; all indicate a drier style of wine.

June's Picks

I love doing tastings of Rieslings from a variety of wine-growing areas, because this wine shows off its terroir big-time. We'll taste wines from the superstar regions of Alsace and Mosel-Saar-Ruwer, as well as from my favorite U.S. region for the grape, the Finger Lakes of Upstate New York, and one from California.

Mosel-Saar-Ruwer Kabinett, Germany ($14 to $20)

Diesel fuel is a strange but alluring aroma that emerges in German and Alsatian Rieslings. The Kabinett, Halbtrocken, and Spätlese all showcase earthiness and terroir that will set them apart from the New World styles.

Mosel-Saar-Ruwer Halbtrocken or Spätlese, Germany ($10 to $18)

These are sweeter styles, so you will smell that in the aroma, and the more viscous body is a giveaway that you aren't sipping the drier, more austere styles like Kabinett and those from Alsace.

Alsace, France ($15 to $25)

These range from bone-dry to sweet, though the majority will be dry and highly acidic. Aromas of grapefruit, apples, and minerals will fill your nose.

Finger Lakes Region, Upstate New York ($15 to $25)

A dead giveaway without even tasting is that many of these Rieslings are bottled with a screw cap. Beyond that, these New World wines have more tropical notes of kiwi, banana, and passion fruit.

California or Washington State   ($15 to $25)

Aromas of fresh peaches, apricot, and citrus are showcased in these
juicy New World Rieslings. These pours will have the fullest body
and boldest fruit flavors of peach and apricot without the bite of the
Alsatian style.

Ringer: Gewürztraminer from Alsace   ($15 to $25)

Another highly fragrant wine made from grapes that thrive in cool climates. Choose one from Alsace, as that region is particularly renowned
for its Gewürztraminer. This wine comes with more spice like ginger,
allspice, and nutmeg, which is sure to set it apart from the Rieslings
you'll taste.

SMELL CAN BE SUBJECTIVE

You're into month six of your wine club. So, how's it going with the name-that-aroma game? Smelling the guava and quince yet? Okay, maybe not. How about more general notes, like citrus, flowers, and berries? Or maybe to you, the wine in your glass still smells like, well, wine.

You'll find that some people in your wine club have super-sensitive noses that really pick up on specific scents, and others don't. Wherever you are on the smelling spectrum, don't be discouraged. It takes a lot of sniffs and sips before you really know how to talk about what's in your glass. You might think a wine smells like pepperoni pizza; someone else might say it smells like cured meat. Remember, it's okay if you don't all smell the same thing.

Smelling wine is all about drawing from aromas you already recognize, so if you're having trouble nailing those papayas and persimmons, go with what you know. When tasting Riesling, for example, maybe a sniff suddenly takes you back to your grandmother's backyard after a spring rain, where a certain sweetness in the air mingled with that earthy smell of those wet stones you used to skim across the canal as a kid. Another sniffer in your group might say, "The nose is all about pears and roses, with mineral undertones." What smells like apple blossoms and wet stones to you may smell like pears, roses, and damp earth to them.

You know what? You're both right. If someone else insists what they're smelling is a rusty hammer and apricot pie, just smile—and keep on sniffing.

This is a great month to talk about aromas. With its seductive floral and fruity notes, this white will definitely play tricks on your nose, but after a few sips you'll understand once and for all that fruity or floral is not always the same as sweet. Now that we're getting into German wines, you may find a new tingle in your nose that reminds you of a gas station. That's right—*diesel* and *petrol* are words you may find flitting around the tasting table this month.

TIME AND TEMP

Riesling and Chardonnay should be handled the same way when it comes to the correct temperature for tasting: When in doubt, chill them out. If you pull the bottles from your fridge at least 15 minutes before pouring, you'll be in good shape.

COLOR Most Rieslings range from pale yellow with a green tinge to a slightly more golden color. California Riesling tends to be a little golden in comparison to the very pale wines from Germany, but they are very close in hue and often there is no notable color difference.

AROMA Riesling is often described as crisp and refreshing even in the nose, but it often includes floral aromas and riper fruits in its repertoire too. Diesel fuel is an aroma that may pop up in German wines, but you may find that note lingering in the juice of Alsace as well; this quality is an earthiness that shows off the wine's terroir. Alsace and Germany will show citrus, especially grapefruit, along with apples, minerals, and a steely, clean nose. You'll find no oak in Alsace and German Rieslings, and I hope none in the others in this tasting either, as Riesling, in my opinion, is too delicate for the likes of wood. California, Alsace, and New York styles may show peach, apricot, and citrus in the nose. The German Spätlese or Halbtrocken is sure to show its sugar when you sniff.

TASTE Riesling should have good acidity and you can use terms like *zingy* or *racy* to describe as you taste. Even though it may smell sweet, if balanced correctly, it should still be tangy or tart. Alsace wines will range from bone-dry to sweet, though the majority are dry and high in acid. New York Rieslings will be fresh with enticing fruit flavor, along with a smoky mineral quality that you won't find in California Riesling. California's will have the fullest fruity flavors—peach and apricot—without the bite of the Alsatian styles. The German Kabinett will be lighter and more delicate in its flavors of crisp apples; both German and Alsatian versions may also taste of citrus, especially lemon flavors. You should be able to distinguish the sweeter German Spätlese or Halbtrocken immediately in comparison to the more austere Rieslings in this tasting.

BODY Remember, high alcohol translates to bigger body. The New York Riesling will undoubtedly be higher in alcohol than the German, and thus fuller-bodied. Alsace versions can range from light- to medium-bodied. The sweeter styles are fuller-bodied and richer in mouthfeel. German Kabinett wines are usually lower in alcohol than the Alsatian wines, so most likely your German Kabinett will be the lightest-bodied of all.

FINISH Some Riesling will go out with a powerful zing, and others may linger longer with softer ripe fruit flavors. The finish should show the acid and leave your mouth watering for more.

JUNE

Recipes

Riesling

LET'S EAT Riesling never seems to upstage the food but instead highlights the best bites. For this month's wine club gathering, you'll love the way Riesling's light sweetness complements so many foods, including the sweet-and-sour dipping sauce and the delicate flavors of ginger and mint in this month's recipes. (By the way, Riesling is by no means a summer-only wine! It's a shoo-in with turkey and trimmings, so remember it during the holiday season too.)

As a side dish or an entrée sprinkled with edamame, these noodles are a family favorite. Mini bites pre-twirled onto forks may look fancy, but they're actually quite simple to put together.

Sesame Soba Twirls with Fresh Mint

MAKES 24 BITES

One 9.5 oz [270 g] package Japanese soba noodles

$3/_4$ cup [195 g] natural peanut butter

3 Tbsp rice wine vinegar

3 Tbsp soy sauce

2 Tbsp sesame oil

2 Tbsp fresh lime juice

1 Tbsp honey

1 Tbsp sriracha

$1/_4$ cup [10 g] finely sliced mint, for garnish

Sesame seeds, for garnish

Cook the soba noodles according to the package instructions. Drain in a colander and cool with cold running water.

In a large mixing bowl, combine the peanut butter, rice wine vinegar, soy sauce, sesame oil, lime juice, 2 Tbsp water, honey, and sriracha. Add the drained soba noodles and toss to coat.

Using disposable forks and a large spoon, twirl the soba onto each fork and place the fork with the noodles onto a platter or individual small plates. Once you have made all the twirls, sprinkle a little mint and some sesame seeds on each.

You can make these ahead and store in the refrigerator (or even keep out at room temperature for a couple of hours) until serving.

Shrimp cocktail served with cocktail sauce is expected. This month, wow your wine club by whipping up this chile lime dipping sauce and taking your typical shrimp to a new level.

Shrimp Cocktail with Chile Lime Dipping Sauce

SERVES 8

½ cup [100 g] sugar

¼ cup [60 ml] fresh lime juice

¼ cup [60 ml] rice wine vinegar

3 Tbsp fish sauce

2 Tbsp minced peeled fresh ginger

1 Tbsp red pepper flakes

4 garlic cloves, minced

2 to 4 Thai chiles, stemmed and sliced

4 tsp cornstarch

2 lb [910 g] cooked, peeled and deveined shrimp, with the tail on, chilled (see Note)

Note: Buy the largest shrimp you can find already cooked. Colossal shrimp are typically eight to twelve pieces per pound. Be sure to have two or three per person.

In a small saucepan over medium heat, combine the sugar, lime juice, vinegar, fish sauce, ginger, red pepper flakes, garlic, and chiles. Bring to a simmer to completely melt the sugar and stir to combine all the ingredients.

In a small bowl, combine 2 Tbsp water and the cornstarch to make a slurry. Add the slurry to the saucepan and simmer for 2 more minutes. Remove from the heat and let cool.

Arrange the chilled shrimp on a platter and serve with a small bowl of the sauce in the center. Alternatively, you can serve in individual coupe glasses with some sauce in each coupe and the shrimp positioned on the side of each glass.

Edamame is an easy snack. Serve with a fun flavored salt, and you and your guests won't be able to stop popping them in their mouths.

SERVES 10 TO 12

One 12 to 16 oz [340 to 455 g] bag frozen edamame in the shell

1 to 2 Tbsp smoked sea salt (see Note)

Note: If you can't find smoked sea salt, you can make your own by combining 1 Tbsp kosher or sea salt and ¼ tsp smoked paprika.

Edamame with Smoked Sea Salt

Cook the edamame according to the package instructions. (I cook mine in the microwave in a covered dish with ¼ cup [60 ml] of water for 4 minutes.)

Sprinkle with the smoked sea salt and serve immediately.

Panna cotta, crème brûlée, pot de crème, mousse, English posset—I love them all. Savoring any of these rich, smooth, creamy desserts always feels like self-care. Here, the flavor is bold like a Key lime pie with an extra kick from the ginger.

Ginger Lime Panna Cotta

MAKES 12 PANNA COTTAS

Two 1 oz [30 g] packets gelatin

4 cups [960 ml] heavy cream, plus ½ cup [120 ml], chilled, for serving

1 cup [200 g] sugar

2 Tbsp ginger paste (see Note)

⅔ cup [160 ml] fresh lime juice, strained

1 Tbsp confectioners' sugar

Grated lime zest, for garnish

Note: Ginger paste can be found in the refrigerated produce section of your local market in either a tube or jar.

In a small bowl, combine the gelatin with 3 Tbsp water and set aside to bloom.

In a small saucepan over medium-low heat, combine 4 cups of heavy cream, sugar, and ginger paste and stir until the sugar and ginger are dissolved. Remove from the heat and add the bloomed gelatin and lime juice; stir until the gelatin is dissolved and evenly incorporated.

Divide the mixture evenly among twelve ramekins, small glasses, or dessert dishes and place in the refrigerator until completely chilled, 2 to 3 hours.

In a medium bowl using a handheld mixer or whisk, beat the remaining heavy cream and confectioners' sugar until medium-stiff peaks form. Top each panna cotta with a dollop of the whipped cream, garnish with lime zest, and serve.

JULY

Rosé

For a rooftop party, boat excursion, the beach, the backyard, and beyond, rosé is here to play. This pretty pour suits the most casual clink to the swankiest soiree. It's like magic—once the weather turns warm, we just switch from water to rosé.

July is the perfect month to celebrate summer water with your wine club. We're not talking about white Zinfandel or blush wine here. Though they may look alike, these wines couldn't be more different. Get ready to get your pink drink on this July.

This month we're tuning in to one of the most misunderstood styles of wine: rosé. Although it's pink in color, rosé is not made from pink grapes. That highly sought-after perfect shade of pale pink, called "pétale de rose," is created from red grapes. Winemakers can use any red wine grapes to make rosé. There are a few different ways to do this.

SHORT MACERATION This is when the winemaker lets the skin of the red grape come into contact with the juice of the grapes for only a short time, anywhere from 2 to 24 hours, to impart color, flavor, and tannins. This is short in contrast to red wines, which typically sit on their skins anywhere from a week to a month. Because the skins are what give the juice its color, this brief contact between skin and juice results in lighter pigment and ends up producing varying shades of pink wine. Most of those ballet slipper pink pours from Provence are made using this method.

SAIGNÉE Coming from the French for "to bleed," this method involves "bleeding off" some of the wine within the first few hours of maceration. This wine is then put into another vat (one of those stainless steel tanks) to make rosé. This method is used to make the top rosé wines from Spain and high-end rosé Champagne like Château Miraval and Cristal.

BLENDING Simply adding a little red wine to a batch of white is known as blending and is most likely the way your fave rosé bubbles (Champagne, champers, sparkling wine, etc.) are made. This method is rarely employed for still (sans bubbles) rosé.

White Zin's No Sin

When many people think of pink wine, their first thought is white Zinfandel. Because of this association, the assumption is that all rosés are sweet, leading to popularity problems similar to those of Riesling from last month. But in reality, unlike White Zin (a.k.a. blush wine), rosé is designed to have less sugar.

Most wine drinkers have probably sipped the infamous pink White Zinfandel wine at least once in their lives. You may love it or hate it, just know this: There is no such thing as a White Zinfandel grape.

White Zinfandel wine was invented by Bob Trinchero of Sutter Home Winery more than thirty years ago. He left the pressed juice of Zinfandel grapes (which is a red variety) in contact with the grape skins for a much shorter time than normal for red wine.

Well, this little experiment (or mistake, depending on whom you talk to) became a runaway bestseller; in fact, White Zin became the number-one selling varietal for a stint until Chard dethroned the pale pink sweet drink.

Why the popularity? White Zin is simple and most are quite sweet, smelling of strawberries, raspberries, and even cream, and Americans like sweet things. For people who aren't used to drinking wine, sweet White Zin is an easy way to get in on the game.

Fancy Bordeaux it's not, but there's no reason White Zin can't have a place in your glass if it tastes good to you. It's relished as a fruity, light-drinking summer quaff.

So if you're going to drink it, drink it chilled and drink it young. Treat it like a white wine: Keep it in the fridge and pull it out 10 to 15 minutes before serving it. This wine also loves ice, so if you like it super chilled, throw in a couple of cubes.

A Rosé Is a Rosé Is a Rosé (or Is It)?

France is home to the most famous version of rosé from Provence. However, this pink pours from all over the country, including the famed rosé from Tavel, just a little north in the Rhône region, and the most affordable French rosés from the southern Languedoc region.

Rosé from Spain is called Rosado and in Italy it's Rosato. The United States makes rosé wines in every region, from California to New York to Virginia. Just as their hometowns differ, rosé styles around the globe range from austere to off-dry and, lucky for us, even bubbly.

What sets the style? Well, like all wine, the winemaker has a heavy hand in what ends up in your glass. The grapes used for this pink drink can be Grenache, Cabernet, Syrah, Sangiovese, Tempranillo, Pinot Noir, Zinfandel, and beyond. You've already been taste testing many of these reds at wine club, so think back to how they differ and you'll see that in their pink versions they vary too.

It's also about the terroir: If the grapes are grown in a cool climate versus a warm climate, the juice will show it. The cool climate rosés, such as those from the Loire Valley and Oregon, tend to have higher acidity and minerality and more tart fruit flavors, whereas rosé growing in warmer climates like Spain and Australia will show riper fruit flavors.

No matter its birthplace or the weather it came up in, the color of what's in the bottle will be a great clue as to what you will experience as you sip. Provence-style pours will be the palest of pinks. This rosé is typically fruity, but it's lean, austere, and not too sweet (a.k.a. dry). Despite its name, this style of pink does not necessarily have to come from Provence, and these paler rosés are popping up more and more outside of the southeast of France.

The darker and redder the juice, the bolder it will be. Spanish Rosados from the Rioja region can be found in much deeper hues, like ruby red, thus offering fuller fruit pours. Be sure to include a darker-hued rosé this month to see the difference skin contact can make.

Rosé can also be savory! Tavel, a region in France's Rhône Valley, produces rosé wines that have a savory quality. They have the same expected red fruit aromas and flavors as their sweeter counterparts, but they can also be salty and briny.

Wine Speak

BRUT Not sweet. A term usually found on bubbly wine labels to indicate that they are dry.

FROSÉ A super yummy rosé wine–based cocktail, served slushy with a straw.

GRENACHE This is the French name for the red grape known as Garnacha in Spain. Both are used to produce rosé. It is also one of the thirteen grapes in the famous red wine blend Châteauneuf-du-Pape.

GRIS DE GRIS Translates to "gray of gray." This is used to describe wine made from lighter pink-skinned grapes like Cinsault, Gamay, and Grenache.

PAYS D'OC You might see this on labels of rosé. Basically, it's the same wine-growing region as the Languedoc region of southern France.

RAMATO Italian for "auburn" or "orange." This is a style of orange/rosé wine made from white to pink-skinned grapes (often Pinot Grigio grapes that stay on the vine longer until they start to change hue).

VIN GRIS Indicates pale pink wine made from red grapes. Just another term you might see on a bottle meaning it's a rosé.

July's Picks

For wine club this month, you'll taste all the popular pinks, including a sparkling rosé. Sip and swirl to see whether you prefer Provence's dry pours or the fruitier, richer rosé styles. No matter which pour, one thing is for sure—these pretty pink drinks are perfect to sip on a hot summer day or as a light, vibrant aperitif any time of the year.

Sparkling Rosé, California   ($20 to $25)

We're aiming for a dry pink bubbly, so look for a sparkling rosé that says "Brut" on the front label or is described on the back label as "dry." Like other bubbly wines, rosé from Champagne will be more expensive than the sparkling rosé from California, Italy, or Spain.

Rosé, Provence, France   ($20 to $25)

The famous chalky, limestone, and schist soil from this region create rosé with minerality. This will likely be the palest pink of the mix and the minerality will be balanced with fruit aromas and flavors.

Tavel, France   ($20 to $25)

These rosé wines are bigger in every way than those from Provence. They'll have a deeper pink to ruby color and higher alcohol; they are richer, with bolder, more layered, complex flavors. These wines can be savory too. This will be the most like red wine of the rosés we'll taste this month.

Rosato, Italy   ($15 to $20)

A vino rosato (Italian for "pink wine") from any of these regions will work for this month's tasting: Abruzzo, Puglia, Sicily, Tuscany, Veneto. Italian rosé can also deliver those savory characteristics we chatted about.

Rosado, Spain   ($10 to $15)

There aren't as many Spanish rosés available, but if you come across one, grab it for this month's tasting.

New World Rosé   ($15 to $25)

Including a bottle of rosé from California, Oregon, New York, Australia, Chile, or basically anywhere outside of Europe will be a great addition to round out your wine tasting this month. This bottle may emulate the Provençal style or it might not. Only taste testing will tell.

Ringer: White Zinfandel from California   ($10 to $15)

This may be a similar color in your glass, but one sip of the sugar-laden juice will be a dead giveaway that it's not rosé.

ANATOMY OF AN ICE BUCKET

If you've ever been a waiter, you know all about side work—all those little jobs customers don't see servers do before and after they sit down to dine. In all my years of waiting tables, it wasn't the pretty napkin folds that stuck with me; no, the most valuable lesson I learned when doing side work was how to make a proper ice bucket for chilling wine.

It's not a matter of just putting ice in a bucket. You should assemble your buckets with two parts ice and one part cold water. This will chill your wine much faster than ice alone; in fact, it will take about 25 minutes to chill a room temperature bottle to the suitable serving temp, compared with the 2 hours it takes in the fridge.

Filling the bucket with both water and ice allows you to move your bottle in and out of the ice bucket easily without any force. Be sure to drape a clean cloth napkin over the ice bucket to wipe the bottle of any dripping water when you remove it.

While we're at it, when serving iced cocktails or drinks, never dunk an empty glass directly into an ice bucket to fill it with ice. Always use tongs, or you risk smashing a glass and leaving the next person with a crunchy cocktail.

Get Your Drink On

Finally, it's time for tasting some summer water. Grab your glasses (with stems), and make sure your bottles have all been sufficiently chilled and are covered for a blind tasting. Take your time and find your favorite pink wine! Happy sipping.

TIME AND TEMP

We've discussed how pink wine is neither red nor white, but at the same time it's a little red and it's a little white. So, what glass should you be sipping from? Rosé can be served in all-purpose wineglasses or white wineglasses. They don't need a big bowl to breathe like a red. More important is that you choose a wineglass with a stem. While stemless wineglasses are great for avoiding spills, without the stem, your hands may warm the bowl too quickly.

Don't let the reddish hues of some rosés fool you—these pinks should be enjoyed nice and chilled. Keep them refrigerated, as you would your whites, and pull them out 10 to 15 minutes before you're ready to serve. Because it's July, keep ice buckets (two parts ice, one part water; see page 164) on hand, especially if you are conducting your tasting outdoors.

COLOR Not all rosé is pink. These wines range from translucent, to yellowish, to peach, orangey, and cantaloupe colors. Some may resemble the inside or outside of pink grapefruit, the many shades of rose petals, pale ballet slippers, and deeper tones of copper, fruit punch, ruby, and salmon.

AROMA Rosés are so fun to sniff. Their perfumes can be sweet and fruity, and have watermelon, strawberry, raspberry, plum, peach, melon, honeydew, and citrus notes. There might also be briny, nutty (like almond), and floral aromas.

TASTE When you sip, fresh red fruits like cherries, berries, honeydew, bright citrus flavors like lemon, and bitter citrus like orange zest can all show up. You might get some hints of sweetness and those savory elements like seaside, minerality, and salinity. All of your pinks this month should taste nice and fresh—no cooked or aged flavors should be present.

BODY Your lineup this month can range from light- to medium-bodied. Because the skins don't hang out too long with the juice, the wine doesn't have a lot of tannins; however, because they're made from red grapes, rosés do have more body than most white wines.

FINISH From your bubbly to your darkest, fullest-bodied rosé, the finish will range from short to medium.

JULY

Recipes

Rosé

LET'S EAT Rosé is sort of between red and white wine, so it can be a pleasant pairing with a variety of foods. Because of the heat that already comes with July, the treats that follow don't require you to spend a lot of time preparing in a hot kitchen. Each appetizer showcases the best flavors of summer. You'll taste juicy garden-fresh tomatoes, radishes, and ripe berries that have been transformed into the perfect nibbles to enjoy alongside your favorite wine this month.

There comes a point in the summer when cherry tomato vines are bursting with fruit, and there's only so many a person can eat. This dip is so simple and requires zero cooking— just toss it all in the blender and grab some bread for sopping it up.

Garden-Fresh Tomato and Basil Dip with Grilled Bread

MAKES 10 TO 12 PIECES

12 oz [340 g] yellow or red cherry tomatoes

$\frac{1}{3}$ cup [45 g] whole almonds or pine nuts, lightly toasted

3 garlic cloves, peeled and smashed

$\frac{1}{2}$ cup [120 ml] extra-virgin olive oil

$\frac{1}{2}$ cup [50 g] freshly grated Parmigiano-Reggiano cheese

$\frac{1}{3}$ cup [4 g] fresh basil leaves

Kosher salt

Red pepper flakes

1 loaf rustic bread, sliced and lightly grilled or toasted

In a food processor or blender, pulse the tomatoes, almonds, and garlic. While the food processor or blender is running, drizzle in the olive oil until it is all incorporated. Add the cheese and basil and pulse several times to incorporate; you still want to see some green flecks in the dip.

Season with salt and red pepper flakes as desired. Serve with slices of the grilled bread.

Making one big sandwich instead of multiple small ones is a time-saver when hosting. It also makes an impressive centerpiece and a filling snack for guests who come hungry. The key to a satisfying big sandwich for a crowd is to use just a few high-quality ingredients and great bread.

Ham and Parm Ciabatta Sandwich

MAKES 10 TO 12 PIECES

4 Tbsp [55 g] unsalted butter, at room temperature

1 loaf ciabatta bread, halved lengthwise

12 thin slices good-quality cured unsmoked ham

$\frac{1}{2}$ oz [14 g] shaved Parmesan cheese

Butter or bibb lettuce, torn into pieces to fit the bread

Spread the butter generously on both cut sides of the bread. Shingle the ham in an even layer across one side, and top with thin shavings of Parmesan and an even layer of lettuce.

Close the sandwich. Using a sharp serrated knife, slice it into 10 to 12 pieces. Serve on a cutting board or long platter.

For this effortless appetizer, you'll make a compound butter using fresh summer herbs (perhaps right from the garden, if you've got one!). I like to serve the butter alongside French breakfast radishes because they have a milder flavor and are long and slender, but any radish will do.

French Radishes with Herb Butter and Salt

In a small bowl, combine the butter, tarragon, green onion, dill, parsley, lemon juice and zest, and pepper. Mash together with a fork until thoroughly combined.

If time permits, spread a bit of the compound butter on the halved radishes and sprinkle with sea salt before serving. Otherwise, simply serve the radishes on a platter with the butter in a small bowl beside it and a side dish of sea salt for guests to scoop and smear on their own.

Note: If you need to soften your butter in a hurry, don't put it in the microwave. You're more likely to melt parts of it than soften it evenly. Instead, try cutting the stick into smaller pieces, then place it in a zip-top bag and pound it with a rolling pin. Use your hands to massage it a little; the warmth of your hands will help soften it. Then, scrape it into a bowl and finish working it with a wooden spoon.

SERVES 10 TO 12

½ cup [110 g] good-quality unsalted butter, at room temperature (see Note)

1 tsp chopped fresh tarragon

1 tsp chopped green onion

½ tsp chopped fresh dill

½ tsp chopped fresh flat-leaf parsley

1 tsp fresh lemon juice

½ tsp grated lemon zest

Freshly ground black pepper

2 bunches (about 24) French breakfast radishes, cleaned, halved lengthwise, and trimmed with a bit of the greens still attached

2 Tbsp good-quality sea salt

Hand pies are the perfect portable sweet. Using store-bought dough is a great shortcut, but if you're a baker, by all means make a batch from scratch before filling. These are stuffed with sweet ripe blueberries, but you can mix your berries or choose your favorite for the filling.

Blueberry Lemon Hand Pies with Fresh Whipped Cream

MAKES 12 HAND PIES

1³/₄ cups [245 g] blueberries

¹/₃ cup [65 g] sugar, plus more for sprinkling

2 Tbsp cornstarch

1 Tbsp fresh lemon juice

1 tsp grated lemon zest

One 14 oz [400 g] box refrigerated ready-to-bake pie crust dough (2 rolls)

1 egg, beaten

Whipped cream for serving (recipe follows)

Hand Pies

Line two baking sheets with parchment paper.

In a medium bowl, stir together the blueberries, sugar, cornstarch, lemon juice, and lemon zest until combined.

Unroll one pie crust at a time. On a lightly floured surface, roll out your pie crust into a rectangle approximately 3½ by 4½ in [9 by 11 cm]. Cut that into six rectangles or free-form shapes. Place 1 to 2 heaping Tbsp of the filling on one side of each rectangle, fold over the other side, and pinch the edges closed.

continued

The filling should fit snugly in the folded-over pie crust without any air pockets. Repeat with the second roll of dough and filling to make 12 hand pies total.

Divide the hand pies between the prepared baking sheets. Pierce the top of each hand pie with a sharp knife to create a small vent. Place the baking sheets in the freezer for 30 minutes. From here, you can either bake right away or transfer the hand pies into a gallon-size airtight zip-top bag and store in the freezer for up to 1 month.

Preheat the oven to 400°F [200°C].

Remove the baking sheets from the freezer and brush each hand pie with the beaten egg. Sprinkle granulated sugar generously over each. Bake for 30 to 35 minutes, until golden brown and bubbly. If baking from fully frozen, bake for an additional 10 to 15 minutes.

Cool completely before serving with a dollop of plain or herb-infused whipped cream.

Whipped Cream

1 cup [240 ml] heavy cream

5 sprigs fresh lavender or ⅓ cup [4 g] mint leaves (optional)

2 Tbsp confectioners' sugar

For herb-infused cream, in a small saucepan over medium heat, add the heavy cream and lavender or mint and bring to a low simmer. Remove from the heat and let steep for 30 minutes to overnight. Strain out the fresh herbs. Completely chill the cream. Omit this step if you prefer plain cream.

In a medium bowl using a handheld mixer or whisk, beat the cream and confectioners' sugar until medium-stiff peaks form.

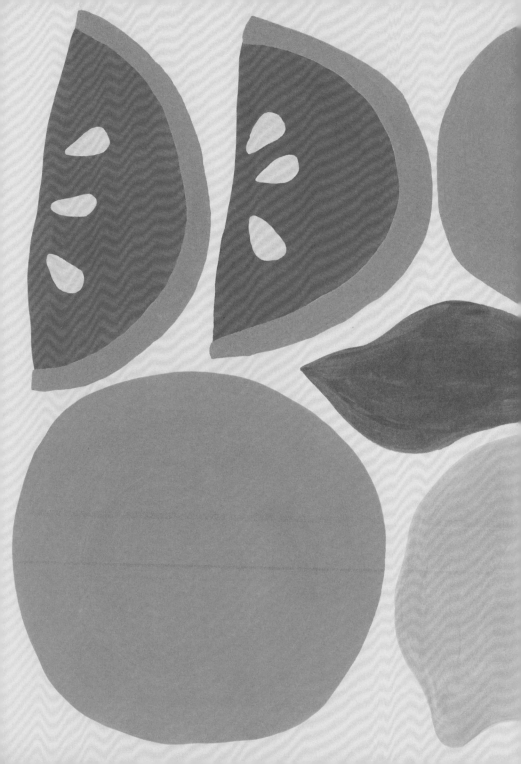

AUGUST

Sauvignon Blanc

chapter 8

The long hot days of summer are the perfect time to get to know your way around one of the most acidic sips in wine: Sauvignon Blanc. Go ahead—take a sip. Wait a minute. Can you feel your mouth watering? That's the acid. And it's so yummy!

Sauvignon Blanc was made for summertime because its acidity makes it so refreshing. (Think about the mouth-wateringly puckery zing of lemonade, and you get the idea.) This month, while swirling and sipping your Sauvignon Blanc, you'll learn other funky little features and flavors in wine that—like acid—are considered desirable.

Getting to Know Sauvignon Blanc

First, let's learn how to pronounce this pour. "Sauvignon" is pronounced the same way as in Cabernet Sauvignon (*sov-in-YAWN*). "Blanc" is pronounced *blahhhn-kuh* (with a hard *k* sound at the end). Be sure to fancy up your pronunciation; that's the way everyone says it—not just wine snobs.

Fumé Blanc (*foo-MAY blahhhn-kuh*) is another name for this varietal. In the late 1960s, when Sauvignon Blanc was considered a lower-quality sweet wine, Robert Mondavi, an American winemaker, began calling his Sauvignon Blanc wines by the name Fumé Blanc. This was to indicate that it was a drier wine in the likeness of those Sauvignon Blancs from France. The "fumé" part of the name was taken from Pouilly-Fumé, a Sauvignon Blanc wine produced in France's Loire Valley (*fumé* is, after all, easier for English speakers to say than *Sauvignon*!). So, if you see it on the label, you will know that Fumé Blanc is simply the same as Sauvignon Blanc. The name has stuck for some American and New Zealand wineries, but in the rest of the world, it's called Sauvignon Blanc. Well, except for in France.

To Oak or Not to Oak

Most California Sauvignon Blanc is made in the Bordeaux style, which means they see oak in their lifetime and are usually blended with another white grape called Sémillon. But for me, the best parts of Sauvignon Blanc—the acidity and crispness—are softened when it spends time in oak. Oak aging means a more timid wine—shy in the acid department, at least. Also, the less work needed (time in the barrel aging), the lower the price of the bottle, so stainless steel–fermented sips are fun for your wallet too.

If you're looking for that citrus rush and read on the back of the label that the Sauvignon Blanc in your hand has even brushed against an oak barrel, put it back on the shelf. Reach for something from New

Zealand, Australia, Chile, or South Africa. On the other hand, you may find that you like the more elegant, rounded-out style achieved by the oak contact. Not sure what you like? Include a California Sauvignon Blanc that sat in oak for this tasting. Then you and your club can decide.

Cheap Dates from the Southern Hemisphere

Sauvignon Blancs from Australia, New Zealand, Chile, and Argentina have fun labels and playful flavor profiles, and they're good values. In fact, you can often buy a variety of bottles for the price you'll pay for just one bottle from the Loire Valley.

While prices for Sauvignon Blanc from Australia and New Zealand are climbing, if you're looking for bargain-basement wines, check out those from Chile and Argentina. Many can still be found for under $15. And do not feel bad about buying cheap wine! Cheap wine is great, as long as you like the way it tastes. I mention cheap, meaning inexpensive, wine when it comes to Sauvignon Blanc from Chile and Argentina because there are just so many!

Of course, once inexpensive wines are discovered to be delicious, you can bet their reputations will spread like wildfire and the blue-light special will be over. So be sure to get in on the action and sip these Sauvignon Blancs while they're hot.

If you are entertaining strictly outside, keep the bottles of wine in a shady spot in ice buckets. But make your ice buckets correctly (see page 164) or you'll learn a memorable lesson the hard way.

Wine Speak

CRISP Describes a mouthfeel and finish that is vibrant and has a zing to it—similar to biting into a tart Granny Smith apple.

GRASSY Describes an aroma that's like freshly cut grass; a "grassy" aroma can also bring smells like fresh herbs or even asparagus or green beans.

SAUTERNES A dessert wine made in Bordeaux mainly from the Sauvignon Blanc grape blended with Sémillon.

SÉMILLON A white grape often blended with Sauvignon Blanc in Bordeaux and California to give the wine a fuller mouthfeel, an aroma of honey, and an off-dry finish.

APPELLATION

An appellation is simply the spot that the grapes you are sipping came from. We've discussed how most French and other Old World wine labels don't say which grape variety the wine was made with. That's because French wines are usually labeled by a geographical name; that is, instead of seeing "Chardonnay" or "Pinot Noir" you'll see "Chablis" or "Burgundy," which are both wine-growing regions, or appellations. That means you can look at a bottle of wine from France, then look at a map of France, and see where the wine was made.

From here, it's easier than you might think to decipher which grape the wine is made from: In France (and Italy and other nations that use this system), wines from a designated appellation must be made from particular varieties of grapes. Chablis wines are always made from Chardonnay grapes, Burgundy red wines are made from Pinot Noir, and so on.

Thankfully, to love wine you needn't memorize appellations and their corresponding grapes. But what you might want to do is learn which Old World (Europe) appellations correspond to varietals (grapes) that you like at home, and vice versa.

How do you learn which appellations correlate to the varietals you love? Most wine shop owners can point you in the right direction—they love to talk about this stuff!

August's Picks

This month, by tasting Sauvignon Blanc from France's Loire Valley, California, Australia, and New Zealand side by side, you'll be struck by the difference a birthplace (a.k.a. appellation: look, you're already wine smarter!) can make. Here are a few picks from each category that will showcase how Sauvignon Blanc shines around the world.

Pouilly-Fumé, France   ($15 to $25)

Named for an area in France's Loire Valley region, these wines are made entirely of Sauvignon Blanc. Fumé is French for "smoke," and these wines possess a pleasant smoky or flintlike aroma. They are more full-bodied than those from Sancerre.

Sancerre, France   ($15 to $25)

Named for an area in France's Loire Valley region, and made entirely of Sauvignon Blanc grapes, this wine tends to be leaner or lighter-bodied than Pouilly-Fumé.

Sauvignon Blanc, California   ($12 to $20)

California's Sauvignon Blanc pours up the signature citrus aromas, but you can also find banana, cantaloupe, peach, apricot, and melon aromas. These tend to be fuller bodied than the leaner Sancerre wines.

Sauvignon Blanc, New Zealand and/or Australian ($10 to $20)

One of my all-time favorite regions for Sauvignon Blanc is Marl-borough, New Zealand. This hot spot blossomed into a wine-lover's mecca when Sauvignon Blanc shot from its stony soil in the late 1970s. It now grows two-thirds of the country's Sauvignon Blanc grapes; these wines provide a perfect introduction to the "citric attack" so loved by Sauvignon Blanc fans.

Chile and Argentina ($10 to $20)

There are great buys to be had from these two regions. These pours will be less in-your-face and powerful than those from New Zealand. They will be fruiter than those from France and more in line with the New World style.

Ringer: Vouvray from France ($15 to $20)

Like Sancerre and Pouilly-Fumé, Vouvray comes from the Loire Valley, but it's made from the Chenin Blanc grape. This is a good chance to learn the difference between the two grapes and get to know another famous varietal from this part of the world. Besides, Vouvray is sim-ply a beautiful wine to sip in summer, so this is the time to explore it. Vouvray wines vary in style, depending on how long the growing season lasts. The longer the grapes dangle on the vine, the sweeter they become. I recommend buying one that says "sec" (dry) or "demi-sec" (off-dry) on the label. Both styles are sweeter than Sauvignon Blanc, so if you detect a sweeter wine in the mix, it's likely you found the ringer.

Get Your Drink On

Go ahead—take a sip. As soon as your mouth starts watering, you'll know why this wine is famous for its acid. You'll be sure to go back for another sip, and another, and another, and . . .

In the meantime, here's what else you may notice.

TIME AND TEMP

Some say Sauvignon Blanc is best consumed within three to five years of the date on the bottle, but mine rarely make it that long. Sauvignon Blanc can be stored (a.k.a. cellared); California Sauvignon Blanc aged in oak and many wines from the Loire Valley have enough structure to hang out for a few years before drinking. But in general, when it comes to Sauvignon Blanc, I say drink this year's wine this year, and next year's wine as soon as you can get the cork out. It's recommended to serve your Sauvignon Blanc at 44°F to 54°F [6.7°C to 12.2°C]. Now, there's no need to be sticking a thermometer in your wineglass. Most home refrigerators should be set between 38°F and 42°F [3.3°C and 5.6°C], so feel free to chill it right in the fridge if you're concerned about the temp. After a few swirls on a hot summer day, your wine will warm up and the aromas will begin to show off.

COLOR Sauvignon Blanc can be as clear as water; in fact, one giveaway that you're drinking Sauvignon Blanc and not H_2O is its those loose, watery legs (what we call the wine drips that cling to the inside of your glass after you swirl; lighter-bodied white wines have looser or watery-looking legs). When it comes to color, a tinge is really all you will see, and a green tinge is a dead giveaway for this grape. Other color-related words sometimes used to describe this wine include green-yellow, pale-yellow, butter, straw, and golden. If it's more toward the golden end of the spectrum, it's more than likely this juice has seen some oak. Whatever the color, the wine should be clear and free of any sediment.

AROMA Across the board, aromas will carry some of this wine's signature grapefruit characteristics, and the wine will be more citrus-like overall than Chardonnay. You may find smoky hints in the Loire Valley's Pouilly-Fumé, due to the soil there. Lemon, lime, hay, green fruit, tropical fruits, mineral, cat pee (yes, cat pee), herbaceous aromas, asparagus, and gooseberries are all common to this grape. And a signature smell of summer is also a signature scent of this grape: fresh-cut grass. Remember this when sniffing and swirling, and you're sure to hear the word *grassy* slide off your tongue when describing this wine's aroma. Sauvignon Blanc from California may emit more banana, apricot, or melon smells. These wines are generally aged in oak and often blended with Sémillon, a grape that adds body and cuts the acidity, usually with a touch of sweetness. Sauvignon Blancs from New Zealand, Australia, Chile, and South Africa will be much greener and grassier than those from France or California.

TASTE As you taste the wines from the Loire Valley and New Zealand, your mouth will fill with a tart green apple flavor. Although you smell citrus, you will definitely taste green apple. Those from California will have you tasting ripe melon, citrus, cantaloupe, and peach. If you sense a taste of honey, that's most likely the Sémillon grape peeking out.

BODY Most Sauvignon Blanc is medium-bodied. You'll notice that the ones you're tasting from the Loire Valley, New Zealand, and

Australia will have a cleaner and crisper body than those from California. Remember that oak thing I told you about with those California wines? Aging in oak and/or blending the wine with some Sémillon grapes gives them more body.

FINISH The acid in this wine can result in a very long finish, but you be the judge. After you sip, if your mouth starts to water, the insides of your cheeks start to water, and your entire palate tingles—this could go on for more than 10 seconds—you've got a long finish. But if the wine feels more like water and washes over your tongue, disappearing down your throat without a trace, that is a very short finish.

AUGUST

Recipes

*Sauvignon
Blanc*

LET'S EAT This month, we'll highlight the acidity of Sauvignon Blanc while taking advantage of summer's fabulous produce. Because it's usually hotter than heck in August, the nibbles I've chosen are simple and designed to keep you out of the kitchen.

Every time I put tomatoes in an olive tray for serving, I get compliments. You can find olive trays at most home stores or specialty kitchen shops. Not only is this another spot to showcase those juicy grape and cherry tomatoes, but it's also a delicious snack that requires no time in the kitchen.

Tomatoes and Sea Salt Bar Snack

Pour a little olive oil in the bottom of an olive tray and place a single row of tomatoes right on top. Serve with toothpicks and a side of coarse salt in a small bowl. Guests should prick a cherry tomato and then just barely dip it into the small dish of salt to coat the bottom.

SERVES 10 TO 12

Extra-virgin olive oil

24 red cherry or grape tomatoes

Coarse salt such as kosher, sea salt, or fleur de sel

Brochettes of Melon, Serrano, and Mozzarella with Fresh Basil

On a skewer, add a piece of cantaloupe, a basil leaf, a scrunched-up piece of ham, a mozzarella ball, another basil leaf, another piece of ham, and another piece of cantaloupe. Repeat for all twelve skewers.

Arrange on a plate, drizzle with very good extra-virgin olive oil, and sprinkle with coarse salt. Cover and refrigerate until ready to serve.

Brochette is just a fancy way of saying "skewer," and this gorgeous assembly deserves an equally attractive name. You will need twelve 4 in [10 cm] wooden skewers.

MAKES 12 SKEWERS

1 small ripe cantaloupe, peeled, seeded, and cut into twenty-four 1½ in [4 cm] pieces

24 fresh basil leaves

6 slices serrano ham, each cut into quarters

12 small mozzarella balls

Extra-virgin olive oil, for drizzling

Coarsely ground salt, for sprinkling

Squash on pizza may sound strange, but this combo of corn, goat cheese, and pesto is stunning. The goal is to keep you out of the kitchen, but if you don't have access to a grill, crank the AC and your oven will get the job done.

Grilled Summer Squash Pizza with Sweet Corn, Goat Cheese, and Pesto

MAKES 1 PIZZA

Preheat the oven to 500°F [260°C].

To make the topping: Bring a large pot of water to a boil over high heat, add the corn, cook for 2 to 3 minutes, then remove and cool under cold running water. Cut off the kernels and discard the cobs. Toss the corn with the olive oil. Season with salt and pepper. Set aside.

In a large bowl, toss the yellow squash and zucchini together with a sprinkle of salt. Set aside.

To make the pesto: In a food processor, pulse the basil, pine nuts, and garlic until evenly combined. With the machine running, add the olive oil and blend until smooth. Season with salt and pepper.

Topping

2 ears corn, shucked

1 Tbsp extra-virgin olive oil

Kosher salt and freshly ground black pepper

1/2 cup [60 g] sliced yellow squash (cut into half-moons)

1/2 cup [60 g] sliced zucchini (cut into half-moons)

Pesto

2 1/2 cups [50 g] basil leaves

1/4 cup [30 g] pine nuts

2 garlic cloves, minced

1/4 cup [60 ml] extra-virgin olive oil

Kosher salt and freshly ground black pepper

To Assemble

Semolina flour, for the pizza peel

1 lb [455 g] store-bought pizza dough, thawed, or 2 large flatbreads

4 oz [115 g] goat cheese, crumbled

1 Tbsp extra-virgin olive oil

$1/4$ cup [5 g] thinly sliced basil leaves

To assemble the pizza: Sprinkle a pizza peel with a generous amount of semolina flour to prevent sticking. Stretch the pizza dough into a 14 to 16 in [35.5 to 40.5 cm] circle and place it on the prepared pizza peel.

If baking: Prebake in the oven for 10 minutes until lightly golden (the pizza will not be cooked through yet). Remove from the oven and spread the pesto over the surface, leaving a 1 in [2.5 cm] border uncovered, then arrange the squash, corn, and goat cheese evenly on top of the pesto. Bake until the cheese is melted, about 10 minutes.

If grilling: Preheat the grill to high heat and lightly grease the grates with vegetable oil. Shimmy the stretched dough off the pizza peel directly onto the hot grates. Close the lid and grill for two to four minutes until the dough starts to puff up and is lightly golden brown on the bottom. Remove from the grill and flip over to add toppings to the cooked side, as directed above. Return to the grill and close the lid for 3 to 5 minutes until the cheese is melty, the squash is lightly browned, and the crust is completely browned on the bottom.

Finish the pizza with a drizzle of olive oil. Garnish with the basil. Cut the pizza into 10 pieces and serve.

If ever there were an adult water ice, this is it. Granitas don't require any special equipment like an ice cream maker— your blender does all the hard work. You can portion these into dessert cups (or better yet, Champagne coupes or dessert wineglasses) for an impressive presentation.

Spicy Pineapple and Mango Granita

In a small saucepan over medium heat, combine 1 cup [240 ml] water, the sugar, and serrano pepper and bring to a simmer for 5 minutes. Strain and discard the serrano.

Place the syrup into a blender with the pineapple and lime juice. Purée until smooth.

In a separate bowl, combine the mango, salt, and chili powder.

Pour the puréed mixture into a 9 by 13 in [23 by 33 cm] baking dish. Fold in the seasoned mango and place the dish into the freezer. After 45 minutes, use a fork to scrape the mixture and place it back into the freezer. Keep scraping every 30 minutes until it is completely frozen and icy—this can take up to 2½ hours. It can be stored up to 4 weeks in a freezer-safe container in the freezer.

SERVES 10 TO 12

½ cup [100 g] sugar

1 serrano pepper, stemmed and halved lengthwise

2½ cups [350 g] fresh pineapple chunks (about 1 large ripe pineapple, peeled, cored, and chopped)

2 Tbsp fresh lime juice, strained

1½ cups [210 g] finely diced fresh mango

½ tsp coarsely ground salt

½ tsp chili powder

The ultimate summer dessert is strawberry shortcake. This one subs shortbread for cake and keeps your oven off. In-season, sweet strawberries are key for this dessert. If they are not sweet and ripe, skip this dessert and make something else.

MAKES 12 CAKES

1 cup [240 ml] heavy cream

1 tsp vanilla extract

1 Tbsp confectioners' sugar

12 shortbread cookies

Balsamic glaze, for drizzling (see Note)

12 small or 6 large strawberries, cored and sliced

Note: Balsamic glaze is simply balsamic vinegar that has been reduced by half to the consistency of molasses. Either use store-bought glaze or make your own.

Strawberry Shortcakes with Vanilla Cream and Balsamic Syrup

In a medium bowl using a handheld electric mixer or a whisk, whip the heavy cream, vanilla, and confectioners' sugar until medium-stiff peaks form.

Place 1 Tbsp of the whipped cream on each shortbread cookie. Drizzle the balsamic glaze on top. Shingle the sliced strawberries on top of the cream. Serve immediately with the extra whipped cream in a bowl alongside, or store in the refrigerator for up to 2 hours until ready to serve.

SEPTEMBER

Natural Wines

chapter 9

September signifies a transition from summer's carefree days to a more structured fall routine. The sun sets earlier, we trade in our flip-flops for socks and shoes, and summer's vibes slowly fade. So this month, for some added fun, wine club will wind down with some weird and wild natural wines.

This is a wine category for nonconformist wine drinkers. It's not a new idea; in fact, its focus on minimal intervention production (from both man and machine) is ancient. These days, the category has a culture all its own, amplified by its quirky social circle of hipsters, artists, and chefs. Beyond the taste of these esoteric wines, they are just as much ignited by the thrill of the hunt for these oddball bottles. It's kind of an underground wine cult and now you're going to be part of it. Get ready to do a little research, some wine hunting of your own, and perhaps even some online shopping. So buckle up: This month's wine club is going to get weird.

Getting to Know Natural Wine

"Natural wine." Sound strange? That's because it is. It's a confusing term for a confusing category of wine. True, all wine starts with nature—plants, soil, rain, and a little sunshine (a.k.a. terroir), et voilà, you've got the makings of wine. So, that's what natural wine is. The motto of natural wine is nothing added, nothing taken away.

Most wine you've sipped so far this year has had some intervention from a winemaker before it gets to your glass. Technically and legally, there are dozens and dozens of additives (seventy-six approved by the FDA, to be exact) that can be included in your wine. Then it's manipulated in all sorts of ways using modern technology and machines. One common process wine goes through is "clarifying," also known as "fining" or "filtering." This essentially makes it suitable for us (the general population of wine drinkers) to sip. These processes take out all the gunk so what we finally see is clear and clean looking, without any floaters. But with natural wines, cloudy is totally fine and the flaws are part of the fun.

So what actually makes a wine "natural"? These are the two main things to remember:

1. They will always be free from additives and chemicals.
2. There is no technological manipulation involved in the winemaking process.

Look at Me

Don't be surprised if you head to your regular wine shop this month and find there is *no* natural wine section. Higher-end, more curated wine shops will have a bigger selection, but most stores only carry a handful of these wines. When you do find them, the first thing you might notice is the array of super-cool, art-inspired, free-spirited labels. Some will say "natural wine" right on the label, or if your wine shop has an organic section, you may get lucky there. Many bottles don't have any information—just an image, or a handwritten label that simply says "wine." There's no holding your hand from the winemakers; it's kind of a trust fall. The way they see it is, if they put it in the bottle, you should try it. Basically, don't overthink your drinks.

After you find a bottle to try, it's time to see what all the hype is about. Descriptors for natural wine include the typical wine color variations we've discussed in months past, but you'll also want to add terms like cloudy, brown, and oxidized (see page 96) to your arsenal for this month's tasting. Brown-colored wine *usually* means bad wine but, in this case, those brownish hues are not an indicator of cooked wine (see page 49). Cloudy is common here, but they can be bottled clear if a winemaker chooses to let the cloudy part naturally fall to the bottom before bottling. And many natural wines can resemble the other wines you've been sipping.

From the labels to the tasting, you might notice that grace, manners, and protocol aren't top priorities for natural wines. But the ritual, romance, and mystique of wine are alive and well in these vin vivants.

Meet the Grapes

More than any other category of wine, natural wines will introduce you to lesser-known grape varieties. Names like Carignan, Charbono, Cartoixà Vermell, Godello, Mauzac, Malagousia, Nascetta . . . basically any grape you've never heard of before is game. In addition to bringing back forgotten grapes, natural wines are bringing light and love back to historic vineyards from all over the world. Because of the growth in this category, New York, California, Australia, Chile, the Czech Republic, Georgia, Slovenia, Spain, Germany, Austria, Italy, and France, among many other locales, are rediscovering and protecting grapes that might otherwise have gone extinct.

Drink Me

When exploring natural wines, you may feel a little bit like Alice in Wonderland with her tiny bottle that says, "Drink Me." For these pours, that's all the instruction you need—there is no standard, so there is no wine for comparison. While the winemaking takes a "less is more" approach, natural wines require a very hands-on winemaking practice.

ORGANIC VS. NATURAL   Natural wine is organic, meaning it is made from grapes that are farmed without chemicals and pesticides. To be labeled "organic" also requires that all ingredients used in the winemaking process, including yeast, are organically grown. Also, no additional sulfites (a common preservative used in winemaking) may be added. However, not all organic wines are natural wines. The difference is that organic wine can be subjected to large-scale processing techniques, which natural wines are not. With natural wine, the goal is to have as little human intervention as possible.

BIODYNAMIC VS. NATURAL   Biodynamic winemaking is a holistic method that views the farm as a whole and also depends on the moon and the stars. Biodynamic farming follows what's called the "biodynamic calendar," where the days coincide with the elements: earth, fire, air, and water. The days are then assigned farming tasks, including fruit days (best for harvesting), root days (time to prune), leaf days (time to water), and flower days (letting the vineyard rest). In order to be certified biodynamic, no synthetic chemicals, including herbicides or pesticides, can be used in the vineyard and no acid, sugar, or enzymes can be used in the winemaking process. All biodynamic wines are organic, but not all are natural. Once biodynamic wines are harvested, they can employ technology in the winemaking process.

The gist of this is all natural wines are organic and may be biodynamic, but organic and biodynamic wines are not necessarily natural.

Debunking Au Natural Myths

Myth #1

NATURAL WINE IS HEALTHY. There are fewer chemicals and additives in natural wine—they are lower in sugar, can be vegan, can fit a paleo or keto diet, can be lower in alcohol. So, these pours can be a better option depending on your definition of "healthy." For those with a sulfur allergy or intolerance, natural wines are low in sulfites (note that if you can eat dried fruit, you're not allergic to sulfites), but note that all wine naturally contains sulfites from fermentation.

Myth #2

ALL NATURAL WINE TASTES LIKE CIDER. Some natural wines taste just like regular ol' wines. Because of the slower fermentation of natural wine, those sour, cider/kombucha-esque characteristics are common, but as mentioned, nothing can be overarchingly applied to all of the wines in this category, except that they will all be unique.

Myth #3

NATURAL WINE IS ALL LOW ABV (ALCOHOL BY VOLUME). Some are as low as 3 percent ABV, but usually the range falls between 9 and 11 percent. Most white wine you've tasted has probably been 11 to 12 percent, and some reds like big Zins can show up higher, like 13 to 14 percent. So, while some of the au natural sips can be very low ABV, most are pretty close to the norm.

FREE THE GRAPES

Because natural wines can be elusive, online shopping this month may be your safest and quickest bet to stock up. However, it is not legal to ship to all fifty states. A movement called Free the Grapes (freethegrapes.org) keeps track of the laws, helps lobby for direct wine shipping everywhere, and ensures consumer choice when it comes to buying wine. At the time of writing this book, it was not permitted to ship directly to your door if you live in Alabama, Mississippi, Utah, and Kentucky, with restricted shipping laws in place in Rhode Island, Delaware, New Jersey, and Louisiana. Though it may be legal to ship to your state, a lot of online wine shops won't (including Amazon, which only ships to very select locations).

Once you figure out whether it's legal for you to order wine, you can easily do a Google search for natural wine or check out one of these recommended natural wine shops:

DRYFARMSWINE.COM This is a wine club for natural wine. You pick your color—red, white, or rosé—and they ship it to you with their guarantee that you're going like them.

NATURALWINE.COM If you don't want to join a monthly club, you can find a great selection in every category from around the world here.

WINE.COM The selection is not huge, but the prices are right, and with demand will come more options.

UNROOTEDWINES.COM These guys do the wine hunting for you and offer an interesting selection of hard-to-find natural wines.

GOODCLEAN.WINE From the minds of a former beauty, health, and fitness editor and an aesthetician come these better-for-you wines delivered right to your door.

September's Picks

For this month's wine tasting, we'll include a red, a white, a rosé, an orange, and a Pét-Nat. If you can't locate one of each of these, then just focus on trying five different natural wines. That can include a couple of one of these categories as long as they are all different, whether it be grapes or producers. The prices for natural wine can range from $10 to upwards of $50 per bottle. The goal is to taste a variety, and if one is being recommended by your wine shop, take the recommendation. You already know the deal with reds, whites, and rosés, but here's a bit about the other natural wines you might encounter.

Orange Wine ($18 to $35)

This category of wine is made just like natural rosés, but it's made from white grapes, not red. It uses little to no additives, with minimal intervention in the winemaking process. Orange wines aren't new, but they are having a resurgence. These pours have been around for at least five thousand years and are made all over the world, from Austria to Italy, Georgia, Slovenia, South Africa, and now the United States and Australia.

Orange wine ferments in vats with the stems, seeds, and skins of the grapes. The wines can be big, bold, and tannic, even though they are made from white wine grapes. Orange wines can turn out sour or oxidized (see page 96), and they smell like honey, nuts, apricot, and dried orange. Above all, they look orange or amber in color. These orange hues come from exposure to the oil in the seeds of the grapes during fermentation. Treat this natural pour like you would a rosé and serve it chilled.

Pét-Nats vs. Champers   ($15 to $25)

Pétillant naturel is French for "naturally sparkling wine." They are no-fuss, not fancy, usually cloudy, and slightly sweet wines that are sparkling naturally from fermentation. As opposed to traditional Champagne (a.k.a. champers), which can be abundant with endless bubbles, naturally fermented wines are just slightly spritzy with a little bit of fizz.

Pét-Nats, for short, differ from Champagne in a couple of ways: They don't undergo the second fermentation that traditional sparkling wines do where they get the added yeast and sugar. They also have a funk to their flavor, don't have as many bubbles, and don't have as much alcohol. While all natural wines have some spritz, often it goes away after a swirl or two. (Like all things in the arena of natural wine, there is no rule of thumb.) Your glass of Pét-Nat may have barely a bubble or have a more sustained spritz—there's no telling until you sip. This is not the champers you're used to popping.

Below in each category are terms for you to reference, but if what you see, smell, taste, and experience aren't on this list, that's to be expected. More than specific smells and tastes, these wines have been described as alive, exciting, energetic, refreshing, and vibrant. This month is a testament to seeing how open-minded you and your wine club can be. It's a nice, lightly spritzy reminder to not take yourself or your wine so seriously. Here's to sipping a little fun!

COLOR Pale straw, gold, amber, orangey, pinkish, cloudy, brownish, ruby, ruddy red, purplish.

AROMA Funky, sour, white fruits (like apple, pear, citrus, peach, pineapple, banana) or red fruits (like cherries, blackberries, currants, blueberries, strawberries, plums), smoky or savory aromas like mushrooms or earthiness, honey, vanilla, cream, candy, flowers, herbs and spices from black pepper to cinnamon.

TASTE Bitter, tangy, tart, fruity, minerality, spicy, sour, sweet.

BODY Effervescent, spritzy, light- to medium-bodied, earthy.

FINISH After you swirl, swish, and sip, count silently in your head. Do you still feel or taste the wine 3 seconds after you swallowed or is it long gone? That would be a short finish. Up to 5 seconds is a medium finish, and if you can still feel it after you've read this paragraph, that wine has a long finish.

SEPTEMBER

Recipes

*Natural
Wines*

LET'S EAT This month, our food lineup is just as interesting as all the natural wines we're sipping. From earthy mushrooms to tangy chutney and spicy seafood, this month's menu is sure to round out a super fun and unique wine club. Clink!

Mushrooms are the epitome of earthy, so when sipping wine redolent with earthy aromas, this appetizer is the perfect complement. Mushrooms are loaded with moisture, so the key to getting them crispy is a very hot oven.

Crispy Mushrooms with Smoky Crème Fraîche

SERVES 12

2 lb [910 g] mixed mushrooms, cleaned and sliced

2 Tbsp extra-virgin olive oil

1 Tbsp fresh thyme leaves

Kosher salt

$3/_4$ tsp garlic powder

8 oz [230 g] crème fraîche

1 tsp smoked hot paprika

Preheat the oven to 450°F [230°C].

Spread the mushrooms in one layer on a wire rack set on a baking sheet. Bake for 20 minutes. Turn and place under the broiler for another 3 to 4 minutes, until golden brown.

Remove from the oven, transfer the mushrooms to a bowl, and toss with the olive oil, thyme, salt, and garlic powder.

In a small bowl, combine the crème fraîche and paprika. Serve the mushrooms hot with the crème fraîche alongside for dipping.

Mango Chutney Bruschetta

In a small saucepan over medium heat, heat the olive oil. Add the ginger and garlic and sauté, stirring constantly for 2 to 3 minutes, until soft.

In a separate shallow saucepan over medium heat, combine the coriander, cumin, cardamom, cloves, and cinnamon and toast until fragrant, about 2 to 4 minutes.

Add the toasted spices to the ginger and garlic. Add the preserves and stir to combine. Bring to a slow simmer and cook for 10 minutes. Remove from the heat. Remove the cardamom pods and discard. Stir in the apple cider vinegar and let cool to room temperature before using.

To assemble, spread 1 tsp of cream cheese on each baguette slice. Top each with 1 tsp of chutney and serve on a platter.

I love Indian cuisine, mostly because the layers of spice and aromatics are so warm and inviting. As you cook this homemade mango chutney, everyone will flock to the kitchen to see what that amazing smell is. The recipe makes more chutney than you will need, so store the leftovers in the refrigerator and enjoy it on toast or dolloped on vanilla ice cream.

MAKES 15 PIECES

1 Tbsp olive oil

2 tsp grated peeled fresh ginger

2 tsp minced garlic

$\frac{1}{2}$ tsp ground coriander

$\frac{1}{2}$ tsp ground cumin

6 cardamom pods

$\frac{1}{4}$ tsp ground cloves

$\frac{1}{4}$ tsp ground cinnamon

1 cup [250 g] mango peach preserves

2 Tbsp apple cider vinegar

5 Tbsp [75 g] cream cheese

1 fresh baguette, cut into 15 thin slices

This combo of fruit, cheese, and nuts makes the perfect bite. If you have a ceramic egg tray or a platter for deviled eggs, it will work perfectly for serving these stuffed figs.

MAKES 24 PIECES

24 small fresh figs

8 oz [230 g] feta, cut into twenty-four $\frac{1}{2}$ in [13 mm] cubes

$\frac{1}{4}$ cup [5 g] thinly sliced fresh mint

$\frac{1}{4}$ cup [85 g] honey

$\frac{3}{4}$ cup [90 g] toasted macadamia nuts, finely chopped

Figs with Feta, Honey, and Mint

Score each fig at the skinny top with an X. In a medium bowl, toss the feta with the mint. Place one cube of cheese in each fig and press the fig back together.

Warm the honey in the microwave for 10 seconds to loosen. Put the figs on your serving tray, drizzle with the warm honey, sprinkle with the macadamia nuts, and serve.

My favorite sushi place, Kawaii Tori, serves up a spicy kani (imitation crab) salad that my whole family craves. So I created my own version to serve at wine club—and it's a winner.

Spicy Crab Salad on Cucumbers

MAKES 12 PIECES

1 English cucumber, peeled and cut into twelve $^3/_4$ in [2 cm] rounds

$^1/_3$ cup plus 1 Tbsp [95 g] mayonnaise

$2^1/_2$ tsp sriracha

$2^1/_2$ tsp soy sauce

$1^1/_2$ tsp mirin

$1^1/_2$ tsp fresh lime juice

8 oz [230 g] imitation crab, leg or stick style, shredded by hand

$^1/_4$ cup [15 g] panko

1 Tbsp chopped fresh mint or basil

Line a baking sheet with paper towels. Using a melon baller, scoop out the cucumber rounds, leaving a solid layer of flesh on the bottom, to create a cup. Place the cucumber cups scooped-side down on the paper towels to absorb moisture.

In a medium bowl, combine the mayonnaise, sriracha, soy sauce, mirin, and lime juice. Once evenly combined, add the shredded imitation crab.

Fill the cucumbers with the crab salad. Top each with a sprinkle of panko and some chopped fresh herbs. Keep chilled until ready to serve.

The crab salad can be made 2 days in advance and assembled with the cucumbers, then topped with panko and herbs the day of serving.

Cake baking may seem intimidating, but with some store-bought shortcuts, this sheet cake is so simple and makes for a swoon-worthy centerpiece that will have your guests gushing.

SERVES 20

One 15 to 16 oz [430 to 455 g] box coconut cake mix (see Note)

1 cup [240 ml] water

3 hibiscus tea bags

1 cup [200 g] sugar

1 Tbsp fresh lemon juice

3 Tbsp Sure-Jell pectin

1¼ cups [300 ml] heavy cream

¼ cup [60 ml] cream of coconut (not coconut cream)

1 cup [80 g] unsweetened shredded coconut

Note: If you can't find a boxed coconut cake mix you can substitute a boxed white cake, use coconut milk in place of water, and add 1 cup [240 g] of sour cream.

Coconut Hibiscus Jelly Krimpets

Bake the cake in a 9 by 13 in [23 by 33 cm] pan following the package directions. Remove from the oven and let cool completely. Remove from the pan and transfer to a baking sheet. Freeze for 1 hour and up to overnight.

In a small saucepan over high heat, bring 1 cup [240 ml] water to a boil. Remove from the heat, add the tea bags, and let steep for 10 minutes. Remove and discard the tea bags. Add the sugar, lemon juice, and pectin and bring to a full boil until the mixture registers 220°F [104°C] on a candy thermometer, about 5 minutes. Remove from the heat and let cool to room temperature. Store in the fridge until ready to use.

In a medium bowl using a handheld mixer, whip the cream and cream of coconut to stiff peaks, and then set aside.

In a large dry sauté pan over medium heat, toast the coconut, stirring constantly so it doesn't burn. Set aside.

Remove the cake from the freezer and trim the edges so you have a neat rectangle. Using a pastry brush, brush the hibiscus jelly evenly across the top of the cake (you may not need all of it). Spread the whipped cream on top and sprinkle with the coconut. Serve on a large platter or cut into small squares.

Zinfandel

When I put away the sunscreen and start digging around for my traditional fall attire, my accessory of choice has become a bottle of this juicy, jammy, big red. It's officially full-on chunky sweater and cozy jeans season, so let's bring out a big red Zin to toast.

Let's just call it Zin for short, shall we? (And when I say Zin, I'm talking Red Zinfandel, which is not to be confused with White Zin.) Although Zin is often referred to as the all-American grape, it's not exactly native to the United States; how it made its way to California is a bit of a mystery. For a long time, wine experts thought the grape was the same as the Primitivo grape from Italy. But as it turns out, those two are just cousins. After some wine-science sleuths did some fingerprinting, DNA style, they figured out the real Zin grape is actually from Croatia, where it's called Crljenak Kaštelanski.

Wherever it came from, Italian immigrants are credited with planting the grape in California in the mid-nineteenth century, and Zinfandel's popularity soared during the gold rush, when miners were looking for a hearty and substantial quaff.

For decades, Zin was used in blending or for inexpensive bulk jug wines. And though Red Zin and White Zin are substantially different (the red being a big, jammy, serious pour and the white being a sweet, pink, warm weather quaff), if it weren't for White Zin, we wouldn't have so much excellent Red Zin. You see, after those Zin-based jug wines and blends fell out of fashion, the race was on to plant the up-and-coming varietals like Cab and Merlot, and California winemakers were ripping up Zinfandel vines left and right. Thankfully, when White Zin busted onto the scene, that all screeched to a halt.

Now that the White Zin craze is waning, more and more winemakers with Zin in their vineyards are turning their talents to producing killer Red Zins. Good thing they kept those vines! Today's bottles command more cash, and this allows winemakers to invest in the vines. But while bottles can fetch a pretty penny, worry not—there are still some good buys to be had.

Zinfandel Stands on Its Own

Great American Merlots and Cabs are often expected to measure up to grand French Bordeaux; American Pinots often get looked at through the lens of the ever-noble Burgundies. The great thing about Zin is that it's not expected to imitate or aspire to anything in the Old World. In fact, aside from a spattering of patches in South Africa and Australia, few winemakers bother much with it outside of California.

Although there are fresh and fruity styles of this wine, the ones people go nuts for are the deeper, more in-your-face styles. Not for the faint of heart, these Zins are known for their backbone, coming on strong with intense fruit flavors (think of the richness of a juicy plum at the peak of ripeness) and often hit you with a punch of pepper.

You'll find, too, that the Zin drinker is a special breed of wine lover. Many wine drinkers turn to Merlot, Cab, or Chardonnay out of habit; they may have a favorite grape, but in a pinch, most can switch back and forth between varietals without a lot of separation anxiety. Not so with Zin zealots—they're die-hard fans. (They're also easy to spot, because Zin leaves your lips and teeth stained like no other wine!) There's just something about this renegade grape that demands this fanatical following, and this month, you may be joining their ranks.

Old Vines

Zin likes warmer climates, but not necessarily hot climates, which is why the grape loves California. While it's grown in many California regions—Mendocino and Lake Counties, Sierra Foothills, Napa Valley, Central Coast, Central Valley, Bay Area, and Southern California—it's Sonoma County that has time and again shown itself to be one of the finest regions for growing this grape. Within Sonoma County lies Dry Creek Valley and Russian River Valley. To the south is Lodi, and from these regions hail some of the best Zin in the world.

When buying Zin, you'll sometimes run across a bottle with "Old Vines" prominently showcased on the label. This means the wine comes from vines that are least fifty years old—though some are even a century old. By the time vines get that old, the grapes they produce are smaller. But what the grapes lack in size, they make up for in flavor, resulting in big, bold wines. You guessed it—an Old Vine Zin is a must for this month's tasting.

Wine Speak

BABY ZINS These wines are lighter in style and lower in alcohol.

CHEWY I use this term to describe big, meaty Zins. These are wines with super huge body, alcohol, and fruit. They feel like you could eat them instead of drink them (or as I like to say, these are the ones you could drink with a fork).

FRUIT BOMB Term often used disparagingly by wine geeks to describe an intensely fruit-forward wine. Bold, jammy Zins sometimes get this label, but if you like them, that's all that matters.

HOT Describes wines that leave a burn in your mouth and throat when the alcohol taste is too intense and not in balance with the fruit.

JAMMY Describes wines with super-concentrated ripe fruit flavors.

MONSTER ZINS These are big wines. They are full-bodied, rich, and high in alcohol—sometimes as high as 17 percent.

SALTED WINE

When learning about wine, you'll find a lot of the information repetitive, with a lot of wine "experts" saying just what the guy before them said. BUT when you come across someone totally dynamic with something real to contribute, you'll never forget it! This was the case when I met and interviewed the ever-more-eccentric California winemaker Randall Grahm.

At lunch, he pulled a few tricks from his sleeve—literally—to teach me about terroir. Randall poured a glass of red wine. We swirled and sniffed and sipped to our delight. Then he sprinkled a little something into our glasses and prompted me to drink.

When we sipped again, there was a noticeable difference in the wine with the tiny tablets. Turns out it was just plain table salt. Yet, the addition of it to the wine changed the mouthfeel and the tannin structure on the palate. With this little trick, Randall taught me that high levels of sodium in soil can completely alter the final juice. It transforms blocky tannins and gives them much greater length on the palate—and that's a characteristic of Old World wine's terroir.

For a little fun, take a glass of big red tannic American Zin and season it with a sprinkling of table salt. See whether you notice the tannin change. Is your New World wine seeming a bit old school? Sodium is just one of the many elements that come into play with terroir. This simple experiment will quickly show you how one small element can change the entire tasting game.

October's Picks

Frankly, California's at the top of the Zin game, so there's just no reason to go outside of the state for this tasting. Besides, you've already tasted how terroir shows differently in wines from country to country, so now let's see whether you can detect some differences between wines grown within particular regions within one state, and even in particular regions within one county. Here are some options for you to pick your poison this month.

Dry Creek Valley $24 to $35)

You'll want to pick one of the many old vine Zins that come from this region. Full of fruit and softer tannins, an old vine Zin will showcase a big mouthful, to the point that it is sometimes syrupy or really full-bodied.

Russian River Valley or Alexander Valley ($14 to $25)

Zin from these cooler regions tends to be lower in alcohol and higher in acidity. They will be lighter bodied and less concentrated.

Central Valley, Lodi ($14 to $18)

Lodi is home to lots of juicy, bold Zinfandels with balanced tannins.

Napa Valley ($14 to $25)

This region is ideal for growing smaller grapes, which translates to more concentrated flavor.

Paso Robles, Central Coast ($13 to $19)

Ask your wine merchant for a "claret style" Zin—one with less alcohol (12 to 13 percent)—so you can sample a lighter side to this wine.

Ringer: Primitivo from Italy ($10 to $15)

This will be a little trickier to locate in wine shops because it's not as popular. The good news is that Primitivo is generally cheaper than California Zins (you can definitely find them under $15 a bottle and sometimes even under $10), so if you end up liking Primitivo better, lucky you. It is just like Zin in color variation and taste profile. The major difference is that Old World versus New World thing. Primitivo should have that Old World charm and show a bit more terroir and layers of minerality, along with big, bold fruit and spice. It's still high in alcohol, but nowhere near the whopping 15 percent and up for some of the New World styles.

Get Your Drink On

Ready to see whether Zin is your kind of wine? Prepare yourself for an intense, fruit-forward tasting. Because it's all New World juice we're sampling, the styles will vary mostly depending on the producer. So, ask for help from your local wine shop when you're looking for a specific style.

TIME AND TEMP

Like Cab and other full-bodied reds, big Zins should be served between 63°F and 66°F [17.2°C and 19°C]. But don't go bonkers—just aim for room temperature (the variable being the room—lean toward basement temperature, not hot kitchen temperature). However, those fresh and fruity lighter-bodied Zins can be served a little cooler—it won't hurt to chill them just a bit before you uncork them. How do you know whether you have a lighter-bodied Zin? Look at the label—alcohol content (listed on every label) says a lot, and those with higher alcohol content (above 14 percent) are bigger, and those with lower alcohol content (below 14 percent) are mostly lighter.

As for aging Zin, in general, you don't need to. This wine should be enjoyed within three to five years; otherwise, it will lose its luscious signature fruit and just become "hot" (see page 225).

COLOR There's nothing subtle about Zinfandel, especially the first impression it makes. You may think red wine comes from red grapes, but Zinfandel grapes are closer to black, and Zin showcases just how deep and dark the wines from "black" grapes can be. This wine can range in color from deep ruby red to a plummy dark purple (it may even appear black in certain lighting).

AROMA Zin usually brings big, ripe, concentrated fruit flavors, which is why it's often described as "jammy." You may smell raspberry, blueberry, cherry, and blackberry aromas. This wine can be spicy too, so black pepper and nutmeg aromas are also common. Since we're talking about a California wine, you can bet there's oak, so scents of vanilla, smoke, and cedar can find their way into the glass. To help detect these "jammy" aromas, try putting out a few small ramekins of jams, including those from the berries listed above, to smell alongside the wines.

TASTE The hallmark flavors of Zin range from fruity to spicy, so if you like spicy, peppery flavors mixed up with dark cherries, you'll like Zin. In general, the juicy fruit flavors can include everything from blueberry to figs. Of course, there's some chocolate to be had too, you may get a hint of brown sugar sweetness. Zinfandel can also be a bit bitter. Depending on the terroir, you may taste mineral notes. The exaggerated, highly alcoholic Zins can taste hot and will show a more raisiny palate. If you get a lot of layered flavors versus just big fruit, you are more likely tasting the Old Vine Zin.

BODY Zin can range from a soft, lighthearted sip to those super-huge hearty wines. Some Zin makers come from the school of thought that bigger is better, making wines with alcohol as high as 17 percent (most reds top out at 14 percent, and that's usually the big Cabs); in these cases, Zin brings a gigantic mouthfeel. The tannins can also range from softly present to full-blown tannic attacks.

FINISH Big-style wines can leave an unbelievably long finish, but again, some of the softer styles will leave a more soothing feel for the finale.

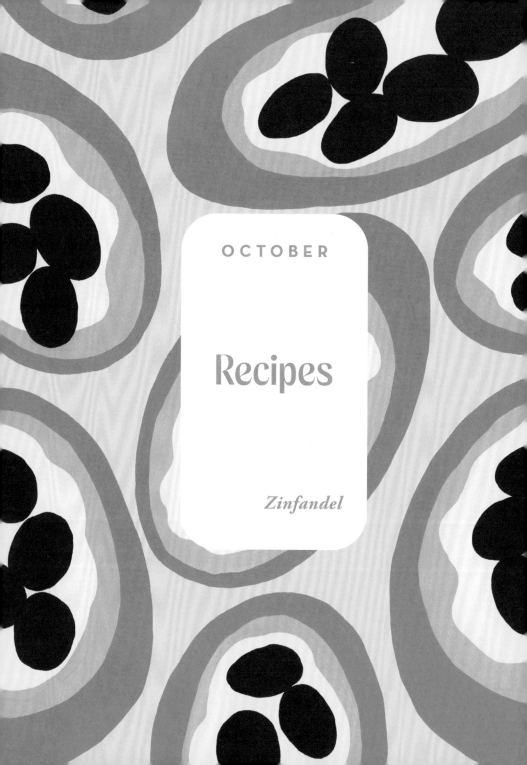

OCTOBER

Recipes

Zinfandel

LET'S EAT   Because Zin tends to have less tannin and great fruit flavors, it can be more versatile at the table than you may guess. Its robust flavors go especially well with tangy cheeses, like goat cheese, and can stand up to cured meats. If you can't get to making these yummy apps below, a charcuterie platter is a perfect option for serving alongside your wine tasting this month.

Big, briny olives aren't just for martinis. For this recipe, I like to use the deli mix from my grocery store, but you can use any mix of jarred olives as well.

Warm and Spicy Olives

In a microwave-safe bowl, combine the olives, olive oil, and both zests. Warm in the micro-wave for 1 minute. If the olives are refriger-ated it may take another 20 seconds to warm through.

Add the feta cubes and red pepper flakes (if using) and toss to combine. Serve warm.

SERVES 12 TO 14

2 cups [320 g] mixed olives

1 Tbsp extra-virgin olive oil

1 tsp grated orange zest

1 tsp grated lemon zest

1/2 cup [60 g] feta cheese cubes

1/4 tsp red pepper flakes (optional)

My bestie and fellow food fanatic, Vanessa, shared this recipe with me. I was skeptical about roasting grapes, but boy was she was right. Don't take it from me—treat your wine club to these sweet and savory crostini and you be the judge!

Goat Cheese and Roasted Grape Crostini

MAKES 24 PIECES

1½ lb [680 g] seedless mixed green, red, and/or black grapes, stemmed

2 Tbsp aged balsamic vinegar

4 thyme sprigs, plus chopped fresh thyme for garnish

5 Tbsp [75 ml] extra-virgin olive oil

Flaky sea salt, such as Maldon, and freshly ground black pepper

2 baguettes, cut into ½ in [13 mm] slices (about 24 pieces)

1¼ cups [210 g] goat cheese, at room temperature

Juice of 1 lemon plus 1 Tbsp grated lemon zest, plus more for garnish

Honey, for drizzling

Preheat the oven to 400°F [200°C]. Line a baking sheet with parchment paper.

On the prepared baking sheet, toss the grapes with the vinegar, thyme sprigs, and 3 Tbsp of the olive oil. Season with salt and pepper and toss to coat (you may need to spread onto two baking sheets to prevent overcrowding). Roast for about 15 minutes, stirring occasionally, until the grapes are soft and the skins start to split.

Brush the baguette slices with the remaining 2 Tbsp of olive oil. Arrange on a baking sheet and toast for about 8 minutes, until golden and crisp. In a small bowl, stir together the goat cheese, lemon juice, and lemon zest.

Dollop about 1 Tbsp of the goat cheese mixture onto each crostini. Spoon the warm grapes on top, drizzle with honey, and sprinkle with lemon zest. Sprinkle the crostini with salt and garnish with the chopped thyme.

Salami, Shaved Fennel, Arugula, and Caesar Mayo Sandwich

This is a take on one of my favorite Italian salami sandwiches. When shaved thinly, fennel adds a great punch of flavor, and dressing the whole thing with a Caesar-flavored mayo makes this sandwich sing. I like to assemble the whole baguette, then place it on a wooden cutting board to serve.

MAKES 10 TO 12 PIECES

½ cup [120 g] mayonnaise

2 garlic cloves, smashed

1 Tbsp fresh lemon juice

2 tsp Dijon mustard

2 anchovy fillets

½ cup [50 g] grated Parmigiano-Reggiano cheese

1 loaf ciabatta, halved lengthwise

1 cup [20 g] arugula

8 oz [230 g] sliced salami

8 oz [230 g] sliced fontina or provolone cheese

1 medium head fennel, cored and shaved paper-thin

Freshly ground black pepper

In a food processor, combine the mayonnaise, garlic, lemon juice, mustard, anchovies, and cheese. Process for 30 seconds. Stop and scrape down the sides of the bowl. Replace the lid and pulse a few more times until the ingredients are evenly combined.

Spread the mayonnaise generously on the cut sides of the ciabatta (you might not need all of it). On the bottom half of the bread, layer the arugula, then shingle the salami, fontina, and fennel. Sprinkle with black pepper and top with the other half of the ciabatta.

Place on a wooden cutting board and slice into 10 to 12 pieces.

ZINFANDEL 10

OCTOBER

My first taste of banoffee pie was on a trip to Turks and Caicos. We laughed at the name at the time, but that didn't stop us from going back for more pie. The combo of banana, dulce de leche, and chocolate shavings felt sinful, just as any good dessert should. These little purses are reminiscent of that pie.

Chocolate Caramel Banana Bites

MAKES 12 TO 14 BITES

One 14 oz [400 g] box refrigerated ready-to-bake pie crust dough (2 rolls), at room temperature

1 banana, sliced

Two 1.7 oz [48 g] packs Rolos

Preheat the oven to 375°F [190°C]. Line a baking sheet with parchment paper.

Unroll both rounds of pie dough. Using a 3 in [7.5 cm] round cookie cutter, cut out 12 circles. Gather the remaining scraps, reroll, and cut out as many extra rounds as possible. You should be able to get 14 circles total. In the center of each circle place one slice of banana and top each with a Rolo. Pull the dough up and pinch together to form little purses. Be sure to pinch them closed.

Place the purses on the prepared baking sheet and bake for 20 to 25 minutes, until lightly golden brown. Serve warm or at room temperature.

NOVEMBER

Pinot Noir

Pinot Noir (pee-noh nwahr) can serve up a disconcerting first sip. Having sipped and swirled some luscious fruity reds like Cabernet Sauvignon and Syrah so far at wine club, this pour, which we'll call Pinot for short, might throw you for a loop, or it just might be the wine of your dreams.

Getting to Know Pinot Noir

Just about everyone who has come to love Pinot has a story. It may not happen with your first bottle or even your fifth. But somewhere along the line, an amazing bottle of Pinot will come along and rock your wine-loving soul.

Or maybe not. There are some wine lovers who never take to Pinot, just as there are wine lovers who never go grapes over Zin, Cab, or Chard. Wine wouldn't be much fun if we all loved the same one, right?

For those ready to journey forth on a quest for a great Pinot epiphany, here's everything you need to know about Pinot:

1. Burgundy is key.
2. Pinot's charms are elusive.
3. Pinot loves food.

Cultivated in France for more than two thousand years, Pinot Noir is often called the "noble grape of Burgundy" because it is the red grape of this world-famous wine-growing area; that is, if the wine is red and it's from Burgundy (or Bourgogne in French), then the grape is—with very few exceptions—Pinot Noir.

Pinot Noir is a bratty grape to grow. It needs a cool climate, yet because it has exceptionally thin skin, it can rot easily in too-cool spots. Pinot grapes require extra care in the winemaking process, and this temperamental wine absolutely must be stored properly. All this contributes to Pinot's spendy price point. But as with most types of wine, there are delish bargain Pinots to be found—you just have to look a little.

The grape is just as difficult to grow outside of Burgundy, and yet, producing a superior Pinot has become a holy grail–like quest for winemakers around the world. Some have succeeded. Outside of Burgundy, the place where Pinot seems to express itself best is in the

Northwest United States, notably in Oregon, specifically the Willamette Valley. Pinot Noir put Oregon winemaking on the map.

In California, Pinot makes up a mere 5 to 10 percent of the total grapes grown in the state; Carneros, Sonoma Coast, Russian River Valley, and Santa Lucia Highlands are known for their divine Pinots.

Soaking in Pinot

Pinot Noir is grown throughout Burgundy, but the superstars hail from the Côte-d'Or, a 30-mile-long, ½-mile-wide swath of land that's divided into two subregions. The southern half—the Côte de Beaune—is most famous for its Chards, while the northern half—the Côte de Nuits—is Pinot Noir heaven. Polka-dotting this narrow bit of breathtakingly beautiful vineyards are world-famous wine-producing villages, including Gevrey-Chambertin, Morey-Saint-Denis, Nuits-Saint-Georges, Chambolle-Musigny, Vougeot, and Vosne-Romanée.

If you want a great bottle of Pinot Noir from Burgundy, all it takes is to choose a bottle from one of those world-famous wine-producing villages, right?

Oh please, it's never that simple.

This moody bunch of grapes doesn't always produce awesome wine even when grown in the precious patches of these world-famous vineyards. Unfortunately, Pinot Noir lives up to its reputation as the "heartbreak grape." It's so difficult to grow, but it's also a heartbreak for the wine lover; you can plunk down some major cash on premier cru wine (see The Crux of Cru, page 243) and be entirely bummed out. Another day, you'll roll the dice on a simple Bourgogne rouge for under $15 that will make you jazzed for the bang you got from your buck.

South Africa makes amazing wines, but not a lot of them hit our shelves. Because we're talking Pinot this month, you may also want to check out Pinotage. This South African grape is no Pinot Noir, but it is related—it's a crossbreed of Pinot Noir and another grape, Cinsault.

It's a meaty red, much fleshier than our delicate Pinot Noir. It is big and chewy and deserves some street cred among the biggest reds. Its dark, inky juice is full of blackberries and currants. This is not a wine for the faint of heart. Look for one from around the Cape, Stellenbosch, or Paarl.

To Blend or Not to Blend

In Burgundy there's no question. The answer is a resounding *no*. While the best wines of Bordeaux are blends of different grapes, white Burgundy (Chardonnay) and red Burgundy (Pinot Noir) are never, ever blended. Well, at least the top wines stay 100 percent true to the varietal. Red Burgundy is synonymous with Pinot Noir, and a white Burgundy is 100 percent Chard. Mention this tidbit at your next office party and you'll seem like a true wine pro.

The Crux of Cru

Understanding how Burgundy wines are ranked in terms of quality is challenging even to veteran wine lovers. Below is a rough guide to the classifications, starting from lowest to highest. As the rankings climb, so do the prices, because the grapes are coming from smaller, more well-defined vineyards, and these precious patches of land are in limited supply. No need to memorize, but if you're watching your wallet, it's worth a once-over.

BOURGOGNE ROUGE These simple, basic regional wines are generally blended from various lots of grapes grown anywhere in Burgundy. "Bourgogne" or "Vin de Bourgogne" will generally appear on the label.

VILLAGE WINE These wines are made entirely from grapes grown in and around a specific village. The village's name will appear on the label.

PREMIER CRU ("FIRST GROWTH") All the wines in this classification are made from grapes grown in a specific vineyard. The name of the village, followed by the name of the vineyard, will appear on the label.

GRAND CRU ("GREAT GROWTH") All the wines in this classification are made from grapes grown in one of Burgundy's highest-ranked vineyards. Only the name of the vineyard (and not the village) will appear on the label. Grand cru wines are extremely rare, representing only 2 percent of the total production in Burgundy.

Vin de Barnyard

Of all the grape varieties, it's most difficult to make flavor generalizations about Pinot Noir, because the wine so transparently demonstrates its terroir; depending on where it's grown, its charms can vary greatly.

In fact, while Pinot is often described as offering the aromas and flavors of bright red fruits, mushrooms, and certain spices, it's more often nonfood descriptors that come to mind when talking about Pinot. Some Pinot Noir from France has lovingly been said to have the perfume of a barnyard. Yes, that's right: wet hay, horses, and straight-up manure. It can also exhibit piney or resin-like qualities, like furniture polish. Top off those aromas with a wine that can taste sour and bitter and make your mouth pucker, and you have a funky wine indeed.

But these are qualities that actually make Pinots complex, layered, and interesting. Often, the juice beneath the odd aromas can be some of the most succulent you've ever sipped. So don't be afraid to sip even if you don't love the sniff—most often, once you swirl a few rounds, this smell will lessen and even go away or "blow off" (see Wine Speak, page 246). If you just can't get over those barnyard aromas, stick to Pinot from the New World, especially California and Oregon.

Wine Speak

BLOW OFF Sometimes, when a wine smells a little funky at first, the funky smell will lessen or disappear after the wine breathes a while.

BRIGHT Refers to a wine that's translucent enough for light to shine through it. While this is usually a descriptor for white wines, Pinot can often be described as bright. Bright can also refer to the taste of a wine—the term applies if the acidity is well balanced.

SHIMMERING Descriptor for a wine that reflects light as well as lets light shine through it.

SILKY Refers to a smooth and rich mouthfeel—often used to describe Pinot.

UMAMI This refers to the fifth flavor (the other four are sweet, sour, salty, and bitter). Umami is an earthy, dirty flavor you get from mushrooms. It's evident in a lot of Asian cuisines and also in a lot of Pinot Noir. It's a terroir taste if there ever were one.

VELVETY Another term often used to describe the mouthfeel of Pinot—it's soft yet intensely rich.

November's Picks

This month, we'll have Burgundy in the mix. Don't worry, I won't have you buying a grand or premier cru. We'll see what the other rungs bring, and whether you can tell a marked difference between a Village Wine and a Vin de Bourgogne. Of course, if you're feeling splashy, by all means, splurge on a premier cru—get recommendations from a reliable wine shop, or try one from one of the producers I've recommended for the Burgundy picks. We'll also sip Pinots from Oregon and California and see what the New World has to offer. I'm asking you to shell out a little more dough on these selections, but I'm having you buy just four bottles instead of five (plus the ringer).

This month is unique in that I'm suggesting you look for specific producers or wholesalers (or negociants, in France) for the wines you taste. In the Pinot game, choosing wines from a tried-and-true negociant or producer is often more reliable than choosing based on village, vineyard, or price. And of course, ask for other recommendations from your wine merchant.

Vin de Bourgogne, Burgundy, France ($18 to $25)

Look for wines from Louis Jadot. The wine will say "Bourgogne" on the label.

Village Wine, Burgundy, France ($28 to $40)

The name of the village will appear on the bottle; these are often hyphenated (e.g., Gevrey-Chambertin, Morey-Saint-Denis, Nuits-Saint-Georges, Chambolle-Musigny, Vosne-Romanée.

WHEN IN DOUBT,
CONSULT THE EXPERTS

Ever settle into a lively dinner with friends only to have the fun hit a major speed bump when that wine list gets plunked down in front of you? Don't feel bad—in my guesstimation, less than 1 percent of diners know everything in there. The other 99 percent are left feeling intimidated, which may explain why easy-to-love Chard and Pinot Grigio remain on the bestseller list. But when you want to branch out, rely on the experts. This is not the month to walk down the aisles of the mega wine store and go eeny, meeny, miny, moe. This is the month to get close and cozy with someone who is familiar with great Pinot.

That someone would be a passionate sommelier if you're eating out or a wine shop owner or manager if you're dining in. For these experts to bring you something you'll love, they need to know a little bit about you. Talk to them. Arm them with some knowledge of your taste buds. For example, let them know whether you like big tannin-packed wines or soft, mellow wines. Sweet or dry? Zippy or smooth? Tell them too what you'll be eating, as they should have a strong understanding of how these wines pair with different flavors.

It's also very important to let them know how much you want to spend. They'll have no idea how much dough you're looking to dish out, so give them a range that looks compatible with the list. A good sommelier or wine shop owner will work with this range, and never try to force a $500 bottle on you.

Pinot Noir, Oregon   ($20 to $25)

Great producers include Domaine Drouhin, Adelsheim, Archery Summit, Erath Vineyards, Sokol Blosser, and Rex Hill Vineyards.

Pinot Noir, California   ($20 to $25)

For California Pinots, finding pours within this price point is more important than finding any specific name. But a few good suggestions are Acacia, Au Bon Climat, Calera, Gary Farrell, Iron Horse, La Crema, Pepperwood Grove, Steele, Sanford, and Tantara.

Ringer: Beaujolais from France   ($10 to $15)

Produced in the Beaujolais region of Burgundy, Beaujolais (*boh-joh-LAY*) is the exception to the rule that all red Burgundies are Pinot Noir, as this one is made from the Gamay grape, which lends a pinkish, pale purple hue to the wine. You might even be able to pick up the famous Beaujolais Nouveau, which is released the third Thursday of every November, and is meant to be drunk very, very young. If you find you enjoy Beaujolais, you might want to consider stocking up for your upcoming holiday fêtes—often you can buy a case of this wine for the price of one bottle of Pinot from the same side of the globe. Make sure you throw this one in the fridge before serving; it shows well on the chilly side. You'll be able to spot this ringer because of the difference in body (it's lighter) and the difference in color (lighter tones). Plus, all those earthy qualities found in Pinot tend to be absent in Beaujolais.

Get Your Drink On

The levels of price in Pinot don't always predict the final product. There's no guarantee a village wine is going to be a lot better than vin de Bourgogne, and a grand cru isn't always better than a premier cru.

When it comes to describing Pinot Noir, sometimes the food comparisons (cherry, blackberry, etc.) just don't do it justice. So, when you're chatting about this grape, don't be surprised if more captivating words come to mind: silky, sensuous, seductive, complex, layered, and so on. If you're at a loss for words, see whether these are some of the attributes you're noticing in the wine.

TIME AND TEMP

Most Pinot should be sipped young. Usually, it has some time in the bottle before it is released to you, so when you buy the wine it's ready for tonight's dinner—or even better, today's lunch. There are some Pinots that can stand the test of time, but five to seven years after the vintage date is a sweet spot. This wine doesn't give the gusto of a big red, so usually a nap in the wine cellar longer than that doesn't do it much good. Yet some producers do say their Pinot can be cellared for decades to come. Whenever you do decide to pour your Pinot, serve it a teensy bit cooler than your big reds. Aim for 60°F to 62°F [15.6°C to 16.7°C], which can be achieved by putting it the fridge for 30 minutes before you pour.

COLOR Shimmery ruby red, velvety, a touch of violet. This can be a see-through red wine that delivers big flavor, so don't be fooled by appearances.

AROMA New World wines again will be fruitier, with notes of sweet red berries, plums, and cherries. Pinot Noir from Burgundy can be barnyardy, mushroomy, earthy, and musty. American Pinot shows its oak, so look for that creamy vanilla. Both new and old can include a hint of smoke, leather, herbs like rosemary and thyme, and scents of pine, eucalyptus, and peppermint. Floral aromas can include lilacs, roses, and violets.

TASTE French Pinot tends to be less alcoholic, lighter-bodied, and more subtle and earthy than American Pinot. American Pinots are bigger, bolder, and more fruit-forward. While Old World Pinot shows its earth, American Pinot shows its oak with a ripple of sweet spices. The fruits of this wine are usually red berries like strawberries, raspberries, and cranberries.

BODY Pinot is one of the lightest-bodied reds we've sipped thus far; it's softer than big Cabs and has more finesse than Merlot. Pinot is silky, smooth, and melts in your mouth—instead of storming it.

FINISH Its color may not be brash, but the finish of Pinot can be big. Pinot's light tannins and bright acidity make for a mouthwatering finish that will have you begging for more.

NOVEMBER

Recipes

Pinot
Noir

LET'S EAT   The great thing about Pinot is that it rarely lets you down in the food-and-wine pairing department. In fact, Oregon's Pinots were the first to break the hallowed and predictable rule: "Red with meat; white with fish and poultry." These wines are flexible and can go with both. They have good acidity and are loaded with fruit flavor, two attributes of a food-loving wine. Of course, you can't go wrong with dishes specifically created for Burgundy wines: coq au vin and boeuf Bourguignon. However, because it's November, for this tasting, let's think Thanksgiving. So, after the family has packed up and left, let's transform those leftovers into delicious hors d'oeuvres.

"Nooch" is the abbreviated name for nutritional yeast, a nutty, cheesy-flavored seasoning that is often used as a dairy alternative. This ingredient is a game changer in salad dressings, sauces, and anything that could benefit from a salty, umami boost, like this buttery popcorn.

Rosemary Nooch Popcorn

SERVES 12

5 Tbsp [75 g] salted butter

1 tsp cayenne pepper

4 Tbsp [5 g] chopped fresh rosemary, plus sprigs for garnish

12 cups [360 g] plain popped popcorn (no salt or butter)

⅓ cup [7 g] nutritional yeast (a.k.a. nooch), for sprinkling

Salt

In a sauté pan over medium heat, combine the butter, cayenne, and rosemary and cook, stirring continuously, until the butter is melted and you can smell the rosemary, about 2 minutes.

In a large bowl, using your hands, toss the popcorn and the melted rosemary butter to evenly coat. Generously sprinkle the nutritional yeast over the popcorn as you toss. Season with salt.

Garnish the bowl of popcorn with sprigs of fresh rosemary and serve.

By far, this appetizer is the one that I get the most requests for. If you're short on time you can use store-bought cranberry sauce, but it's much more flavorful if you make it yourself.

Cranberry Bruschetta

MAKES 12 TO 16 TOASTS

1 baguette, cut on the bias into ¹/₂ in [13 mm] slices

2 Tbsp unsalted butter, melted

²/₃ cup [100 g] diced red onion

¹/₂ cup [120 ml] rice wine vinegar

¹/₃ cup [65 g] sugar

2 Tbsp pickled ginger, roughly chopped, or 1 Tbsp grated peeled fresh ginger

¹/₂ tsp red pepper flakes

¹/₂ tsp minced fresh rosemary, plus whole leaves for garnish

1 cup [240 g] cranberry sauce, homemade (recipe follows) or store-bought

4 oz [115 g] cream cheese

Preheat the oven to 375°F [190°C].

On a baking sheet, arrange the baguette slices in a single layer and brush lightly with the melted butter. Bake for 8 minutes, or until golden and toasted. Remove from the oven and set aside to cool.

In a heavy-bottom saucepan over medium-high heat, combine the red onion, vinegar, sugar, pickled ginger, and red pepper flakes. Simmer until the vinegar is reduced by more than half and the sugar begins to caramelize (the red onion will become pink and translucent). Lower the heat and stir in the minced rosemary and cranberry sauce. Return to a boil, then remove from the heat and let cool completely.

To assemble the bruschetta, smear each toast with approximately 1 Tbsp of cream cheese, top with 1 to 2 heaping Tbsp of cranberry sauce, and garnish each with rosemary leaves.

**MAKES ABOUT 3 CUPS
[750 G]**

1 cup [140 g] fresh
cranberries, picked over
for stems and rotten
berries

½ cup [100 g] sugar

1½ tsp grated orange zest

Cranberry Sauce

In a heavy-bottom saucepan over high heat, combine the cranberries, sugar, ½ cup [120 ml] water, and the orange zest and bring to a boil, stirring occasionally. Lower the heat to medium and simmer until the cranberries have popped. Keep stirring as needed to prevent the sugar from sticking or burning on the bottom of the pan. Cook until the sauce has thickened and coats the back of a wooden spoon.

Remove from the heat and transfer to a heat-proof container.

Let cool and refrigerate, covered, for up to 1 week.

If you don't have any leftover turkey to use in these pot stickers, chicken works just as well. Pinot is usually lower in alcohol and can take a little spice, so try a sip while you eat and see how it measures up.

Turkey Pot Stickers with Chili Oil

MAKES 30 TO 35 DUMPLINGS

In a medium bowl, combine the turkey, stuffing, green onion, egg white, sesame oil, soy sauce, ginger, pepper, and salt. Mix with a wooden spoon or fork until well combined.

Set a large pot of water to boil over high heat.

On a clean work surface, lay out several wonton wrappers and a small bowl of water. With the tip of your finger or a small pastry brush, very lightly brush some water along the edges of each wonton wrapper (this will help the wrapper stick together tightly once you start forming the dumplings).

In the middle of each wrapper place a small mound of the filling, about 1 Tbsp, and fold the wonton in half to make a half-moon or tri-angle depending on the shape of your wonton wrapper. Gently press out any air from around the filling and seal the edges of the dumpling

1¼ cups [210 g] finely chopped cooked turkey

½ cup [100 g] prepared stuffing

½ cup [24 g] sliced green onion, green tops only

1 egg white, lightly beaten

2 Tbsp toasted sesame oil

2 tsp soy sauce or tamari

2 tsp minced or grated peeled fresh ginger

½ tsp freshly ground black pepper

¼ tsp coarsely ground salt

One 12 oz [340 g] package refrigerated or frozen wonton wrappers, round or square

Vegetable or peanut oil, for frying

Toasted sesame seeds, for garnish

½ cup [120 ml] chili oil, for drizzling or dipping

well by pinching together with your fingertips. Continue until all the filling and/or all the wrappers have been used up. At this point, the dumplings could be frozen in a single layer and reserved for future use.

Once the water is at a rapid boil, drop in several of the dumplings at once and stir so that they do not stick together or to the bottom. They will be done once they rise to the surface of the water. Remove from the water with a slotted spoon or spider and set aside on a plate. At this point, the dumplings could be set aside to cool and stored in a covered container in the fridge until ready to pan-fry and serve.

Heat a nonstick sauté pan over medium-high heat and add about 1 Tbsp vegetable oil. Add as many dumplings as will fit without crowding them. Fry the dumplings for several minutes on each side until golden and crisp. Continue until all the dumplings are pan-fried.

Sprinkle with the toasted sesame seeds. Either drizzle with chili oil or serve the chili oil on the side in a small dish with a small serving spoon.

Gorgonzola, which tends to be a little bit milder than other blue cheeses, is perfectly paired with ripe pears for this pizza. It's even better when served with a glass of Pinot Noir.

Pear and Gorgonzola Pizza

MAKES 1 PIZZA

1 lb [455 g] store-bought pizza dough

Olive oil, for brushing

2 large ripe Bartlett pears, cored and thinly sliced (about 3 cups [420 g])

5 oz [140 g] Gorgonzola cheese, crumbled

Preheat a pizza stone in the oven to 400°F [200°C]. If you don't have a pizza stone, you can use a baking sheet.

On a pizza peel or rimless baking sheet, stretch out the dough to fit your peel or baking sheet (it can be round or rectangular), and brush with olive oil. Shingle the pear slices over the dough, sprinkling the Gorgonzola cheese in between slices. Slide the pizza onto the pre-heated stone or baking sheet. Bake for 20 to 25 minutes, or until the crust is golden.

Remove from the oven and allow to cool slightly before slicing.

Parfaits make for such fun party food simply because those layers look so good. This one captures the flavors of fall, and so perfectly complements wine club when served in wineglasses. You could also use two partial leftover pies and make half of the parfaits with, for example, apple pie filling and the other half with pumpkin pie filling.

MAKES 10 SMALL PARFAITS

One 8 or 9 in [20 or 23 cm] prepared pumpkin pie

2 cups [480 g] good-quality sour cream

¼ cup [60 ml] good-quality maple syrup

2 Tbsp orange juice concentrate (from the can)

½ tsp pumpkin pie spice

2 cups [200 g] whipped cream

¾ cup [90 g] crumbled graham crackers

Zest from 1 orange, cut into thin strips

Pumpkin Pie Parfaits

Remove the filling from the crust of the pie. Discard or snack on the crust.

In a medium bowl, whisk together the sour cream, maple syrup, orange juice concentrate, and pumpkin pie spice.

In the bottom of each glass, place about 2 to 3 Tbsp of pie filling. Next, spoon a layer of sour cream mixture into each glass, then add a layer of whipped cream. Repeat each layer until the glasses are full. Top with a sprinkle of graham cracker crumbs and a strip of orange zest.

Serve immediately or keep in the refrigerator up to 4 hours, or overnight.

Bubbles

Popping bottles is not just for weddings or New Year's Eve. Champagne and sparkling wines are perfect all year long and always guarantee a good time. That makes them the perfect pick to celebrate a year of wine club.

Really, how much do you need to know to enjoy Champagne? You've probably already raised a glass or two in your life and had a fine old time with it whether or not you could pinpoint Champagne on a map (yes—it's a place). Ready to delve a little deeper? Here's your crash course.

The Word on Champagne

Ever notice how sometimes wines that bubble are called Champagne, and other times they're called sparkling wine or even something else? Any wine that sparkles can be called sparkling wine, but not all wine that sparkles can be called Champagne. Technically, to be called Champagne—with that all-important capital *C*—the bubbly must come from Champagne, a region in the northeast of France. So out of respect (and because French Champagne makers tend to get a li'l bit territorial about these things), we call all other bubblies "sparkling wines." Specific sparkling wines from other parts of the world go by different monikers, including:

CAVA Bubbly from Spain

PROSECCO Italian bubbly

VIN MOUSSEUX French sparkling wines produced outside the Champagne region

SPUMANTE Fully sparkling bubbly from Italy

FRIZZANTE Lightly sparkling bubbly from Italy

SEKT Bubbly from Germany

SPARKLING WINE Bubbly from California, Australia, and anywhere else not listed is simply referred to as sparkling wine.

Two of the most famous of all French Champagnes are named after people—a monk and a widow. By name, you know the monk, Dom Pérignon, and by sight you probably know the widow Clicquot, or Veuve Clicquot—that bright orangey-yellow label that makes its way to plenty of parties. These two wines are named for people who, as history has it, played major roles in the development of the bubbly we drink today.

Make Mine "Méthode Champenoise"

Sure, now and then it's great to pop the cork on a bona fide Champagne from the Champagne region of France. But if you want some bubbly without spending all that coin, it's easy to find high-quality sparkling wines from elsewhere in the world. If you like that style, it helps to look for "Méthode Champenoise" on a bottle's label. This means that the sparkling wine inside has been produced using the intricate, labor-intensive methods used to make true Champagne. Such sparklers will generally be more interesting to sip than those made by the less-expensive Charmat method (sometimes called "bulk process" in the United States), which involves bulk fermentation of the wine in tanks.

Was It a Good Year?

You might notice that many Champagnes and sparkling wines do not have a vintage (the year the grapes were harvested) listed on them. Such sparklers are nonvintage (NV), which means that they're made of grapes harvested from a combination of years. That's because producers pick and choose among the grapes from a variety of years to achieve the style of Champagne or sparkling wine they desire.

BUBBLES | 12

DECEMBER

Some years, the quality of the grapes is so amazing that the wine-maker may deem it a vintage year and bottle some wines that highlight it. Vintage Champagnes and sparkling wines are usually considered higher quality, and there are fewer bottles, thus demanding a higher price.

If the Glass Fits . . .

Unlike most other wines in this book, the bubblies in this chapter benefit from being served in specific glassware.

THE COUPE Very old-school. Legend has it, these glasses were fashioned after Marie Antoinette's breasts; while that makes a great story, the glasses aren't the best home to showcase bubbles, as the wide mouths let the bubbles escape too quickly.

THE TRUMPET GLASS Sleek, but here you're choosing fashion over function. You want to hold Champagne flutes by the stem (or in this case, a hollow stem); with this design, the wine warms up in your hand and the bubbles escape too quickly from the wide mouth.

THE FLUTE Look for a Champagne flute with a small mouth and a stem that is long and slender. This way those beautiful bubbles cannot escape so quickly.

THE TULIP With its slender stem, good-size bowl, and slightly curved lip, this is the top pick for appreciating the aroma of your bubbly.

Wine Speak

BLANC DE BLANCS This term literally means "white from whites," and refers to Champagne made strictly from Chardonnay, a white grape.

BLANC DE NOIRS This term literally means "white from blacks," and refers to Champagne made from Pinot Noir, a red grape.

BRUT The word to look for if you want something really dry.

CUVÉE Sometimes you'll see "Cuvée" on a label; this simply lets you know that it is a blend of juices and not 100 percent Chardonnay like a blanc de blancs.

DEMI-SEC This literally means "half-dry"—which is really pretty sweet.

DOUX OR DOLCE These mean sweet, in French and Italian, respectively.

EXTRA-DRY OR EXTRA-SEC This, confusingly, is not quite as dry as brut.

MOUSSE The foam on top when you pour the bubbly.

PERLAGE The small strings of tiny bubbles you see streaming through your wine. Think of tiny pearl necklaces.

ULTRA BRUT, EXTRA BRUT, OR BRUTE NATURE This is as brut as it gets—really, really dry.

December's Picks

It's time for a "world tour" of Champagne and sparkling wines. With the selection below, you'll get a taste for the variety of styles of bubbly from across the globe. Include at least five picks from these categories to wrap up your first year of wine club in style. Clink!

Cava from Spain ($10 to $15)

Cava tends to have larger bubbles and fewer strands.

Prosecco from Italy ($15 to $20)

These sparklers can be clear, almost watery, and are less aggressive in their bubbles than California sparkling wines or French Champagne. Notes of peach and apricot are typical of Prosecco.

Sparkling Wine from California ($20 to $25)

California sparklers and Champagne tend to have yeasty aromas of baked bread and end with a creamy, mid-palate finish.

Champagne from Champagne, France ($30 to $45)

Loads of strands of tiny bubbles are typical of Champagne and they can range in color from straw to richer golden hues if they are vintage.

Blanc de Blancs ($20 to $30)

Made exclusively with Chardonnay grapes, these bubblies smell and taste like citrus fruit. They have a creamy mouthfeel.

POPPING BOTTLES

People often talk of "popping a cork," but the downside is you'll lose a little of the bubbly as the cork sails out. So instead of going for the pop, coax the cork out with a whisper—it's sexier and you'll save more of the good stuff for sipping. To do this, follow these steps:

1. **HOLD IT** It's important to be completely comfortable with the bottle in your hands. Grip the bottle in your weakest hand at the base, placing your stronger hand on top of that cork to fight the pressure in the bottle.

2. **PEEL AWAY** Remove the foil from the wire cage that wraps the cork; underneath, you'll see a wire cage and a little round tab. Holding down the cork with a cloth napkin or a kitchen towel, bend the tab down and untwist it to loosen and remove the wire cage.

3. **DO THE TWIST** Tilt the bottle away from you (and everyone else!) at a 45-degree angle. With the cloth over the top of the bottle, grasp the cork with one hand and gently twist the bottle—not the cork—with the other. Let the pressure in the bottle gently force out the cork, and let your cloth catch the cork and any small sprays of foam.

4. **HISS OR POP?** The amount of pressure you keep on the cork will determine whether you create an elegant hiss or a head-turning pop. For a hiss, keep more pressure on the cork as you let it slowly make its way out.

5. **POUR IT ON** We've all underestimated the bubbles in bubbly and ended up with a volcanic eruption. If you want to drink this stuff (as opposed to wear it), pour your sparkler in two steps. Start with a 1 oz [30 ml] pour (called "priming the glass"). Let the bubbles settle, then finish off pouring until the glass is about two-thirds full. This leaves a place for those energetic bubbles to go up before settling down.

Blanc de Noirs   ($25 to 40)

All Pinot Noir grapes in this glass, so expect a fuller-bodied bubbly wine.

Ringer

INCLUDE A NONALCOHOLIC SPARKLING WINE IN YOUR TASTING THIS MONTH. Doing so will help you see what alcohol contributes (besides a buzz!) to wine. Also, it's always appropriate to offer a non-alcoholic beverage for guests who don't drink or who drink very little, and this will help you find a good bubbly option.

Get Your Drink On

To swirl or not to swirl? With Champagne, that is a question. Purists say definitely not, but the truth is after a year of wine club you're probably swirling everything—even glasses of water! So, live lightly and don't take yourself, or your wine, so seriously. Swirl if you want to swirl!

TIME AND TEMP

Most wine textbooks recommend serving sparkling wines at 41°F to 47°F [5°C to 8.3°C], but I would suggest 43°F to 50°F [6°C to 10°C]. The colder a wine is, the more flavors are masked—and you'll definitely want to taste the flavors of your Champagne and sparkling wines.

Keep in mind that most refrigerators are set at about 40°F [4.4°C], so you may need to do some adjusting before you serve your sparklers. If you think they're too cold coming directly from the fridge, keep the bottle on the countertop for about half an hour before serving. Remember too that once the wine is poured, it will continue to warm up as you sip and talk and eat and laugh. So don't get too worried about the exact temperature. Do stop and take note as you sip your wine, because as it warms in your glass, the flavors and aromas change too. (A warning about warm sparkling wine: Do not open it. It will explode!)

Sparkling wines should be enjoyed as soon as you open them. However, if you drink a lot of sparkling wines, you may want to invest in a little gizmo called a Champagne clamshell, available at wine shops and gourmet stores, which will save your bubbles for three or four days. If you're in a pinch, you can also take some of the foil you use for the blind tasting and put it into the neck of the bottle, bunching it up so that it fits in the bottle about 1 in [2.5 cm] down but still hangs over and covers the mouth. This will preserve it until brunch the next day, and maybe even until dinner. If your bubbles go flat, cork the bottle and keep it in the fridge to use for cooking when a dry white wine is called for.

COLOR Sparkling wines will range in color most significantly because of style. For example, blancs de noirs will have a pink tint, and rosés will look pale salmon-colored to pink. You'll notice even the clear or white sparklers will range in color; some Proseccos may look incredibly clear and light—almost watery. Other sparklers, like vintage Champagne, will have deeper golden hues. Also take note of the bubbles—whether they are large or small, or whether there are lots of streams or just a few. The amount of bubbles and their size is really manipulated by each individual winemaker. Not all tiny bubbles are attributed to Champagne. Some California bubblies are just as elegant, with endless streams of teensy, weensy bubbles. And in the same respect, there are sparklers from both France and California that come bearing big bubbles.

AROMA Some of the things you'll smell in sparklers include yeasty or toasty scents, citrus, pear, apple, and florals. Prosecco is often noted for its peach and apricot scent, while Champagne and California sparklers bring to the table aromas of freshly baked bread, yeast, and toast along with fruity aromas. Aromas of dried strawberries, ripe raspberries, and cherries show in blanc de noirs.

TASTE Sparklers show every flavor from citrus to spice and toast flavor to grapefruit notes. The important thing you should look for is that the flavors balance each other and that the sweetness doesn't mask the acid.

BODY Unless they are dessert wines, sparklers should be light-bodied. Other words you may be searching for are clean, crisp, or, my favorite, "twinkly," like little stars in your mouth. Do the wines with more bubbles make your mouth feel different? You'll notice that, in general, the Italian sparklers have less assertive bubbles, while most French and California sparkling wines maintain strong strands of bubbles from your first sip to your last. In general, the more elegant the wine, the more you'll see a lasting mousse and numerous strands of tiny bubbles.

FINISH Bubbly will never linger as long as big red wines. Most will be clean and crisp. Some will linger sweetly and with age you'll find a longer finish. Bubblies will make your mouth salivate. Most Champagne and California sparklers that carry aromas of baked bread will usually end with a creamy mid-palate finish. When thinking about the finish of a sparkler, you should pay attention to how your mouth feels as well as how long those sensations linger.

DECEMBER

Recipes

Bubbles

LET'S EAT Bubbly wine club is a perfect addition to the holiday season, and these appetizers are up for the occasion. Caviar and Champagne are a match made in heaven, and bubbly is the perfect pick to cut through the creaminess of an onion tart or the heat of hot honey. And we'll end with the ultimate bubbly pairing: strawberries and chocolate.

Caviar doesn't have to cost a fortune—there are plenty of domestic styles available that work very well for this appetizer. Remember, a little goes a long way, so no need for a ton of it. One taste and you'll see how this salty, tangy bite begs for bubbly wine.

Caviar and Chips

MAKES 20 TO 24 CHIPS

¹/₄ cup [60 g] sour cream

¹/₄ cup [5 g] chopped fresh chives

1 oz [30 g] caviar (see Note)

Low-salt or unsalted kettle potato chips

Note: If you're in the United States, paddlefish and hackleback caviar are both great for this recipe as they are affordable and domestic.

Serve the sour cream and chopped chives in small bowls with small serving spoons. Place the opened tin of caviar on top of a small bowl filled with ice and place a small serving spoon nearby. To assemble, place a dollop of sour cream in the center of a chip, then a small amount of caviar, and sprinkle chives on top.

"Texas toast" refers to thick slices of what some of you may think of as garlic bread. It's a great vehicle for sauces and is yummy on its own. My version gets a makeover with creamy cheese and hot honey.

Texas Toast with Manchego and Hot Honey

MAKES 24 PIECES

One 11.25 oz [315 g] package frozen Texas toast (8 slices)

1/4 cup [85 g] honey

2 tsp apple cider vinegar

1/2 tsp red pepper flakes

1/2 tsp hot sauce

24 thin slices Manchego cheese

Bake the Texas toast according to the package instructions or until golden brown and toasted. Allow to cool and slice each piece into three strips.

Meanwhile, in a small microwave-safe bowl, stir together the honey, vinegar, red pepper flakes, and hot sauce. Microwave for 1 minute.

To assemble, place a slice of cheese on each "finger" of toast. Arrange on a serving platter, drizzle with the warm honey, and serve.

Think of this appetizer as a charcuterie platter on a stick. You can load up your skewers any way you like, but this version produces a very pretty platter sure to please your guests. You will need twelve 6 in [15 cm] skewers.

Antipasto Pick-Ups

MAKES 12 SKEWERS

12 spinach and cheese-filled tortellini, cooked and cooled

12 cherry tomatoes

12 small mozzarella balls (bocconcini)

1 Tbsp Italian vinaigrette

1 Tbsp grated Parmesan cheese

12 green olives, pitted

12 pieces salami, halved and folded into triangles

12 basil leaves

6 marinated artichoke hearts, halved

6 pepperoncini, halved crosswise

12 black or kalamata olives, pitted

In a bowl, combine the tortellini, cherry tomatoes, mozzarella balls, Italian dressing, and Parmesan cheese. Toss to coat.

On each skewer, thread a green olive, a triangle of salami, a mozzarella ball, a basil leaf (fold in half or ribbon onto the skewer), a cherry tomato, an artichoke heart, another salami triangle, a pepperoncini, a tortellini, and finally a black olive. Place on a platter to serve.

Chef Todd Immel, in Atlanta, Georgia, was the first to make this tart for me. I took inspiration from his restaurant version to make a simple wine club–worthy recipe. A sip of sparkling wine is the perfect palate cleanser after a bite of this creamy tart.

Creamy Onion Tart

Preheat the oven to 400°F [200°C]. Line an 8 by 8 in [20 by 20 cm] baking pan with parchment paper. The parchment paper should be 8 in [20 cm] wide by 14 in [35.5 cm] long and hang over the sides. This will make removing the tart easier.

Press the dough into the pan. Trim the dough so that it is only ¾ in [2 cm] high on the edges. Using a fork, prick the bottom and sides of the dough. Bake for 9 minutes. Remove from the oven and let cool. The parbaked tart shell can be made a day in advance, then covered tightly with plastic wrap.

Turn the oven down to 375°F [190°C].

In a nonstick medium pan over medium heat, melt the butter. Add the onions, ½ tsp of the salt, and freshly ground pepper and cook until translucent, 10 to 12 minutes.

MAKES 24 PIECES

One 9 in [23 cm] premade refrigerated pie dough

1 Tbsp unsalted butter

2 cups [320 g] minced Vidalia or sweet onion (about 1 large)

1 tsp coarsely ground salt

Freshly ground black pepper

2 egg yolks

¼ cup plus 1 Tbsp [75 ml] half-and-half

½ tsp freshly grated nutmeg

In a small bowl, beat together the egg yolks and ¼ cup [60 ml] of the cream. Once the onions are translucent, remove from the heat and add the egg mixture. Stir continuously to evenly distribute. Transfer to a bowl and add the remaining 1 Tbsp of cream, the remaining ½ tsp of salt, and the nutmeg. Place in the freezer for 5 minutes to cool. Stir and return to the freezer for 5 more minutes. The mixture should be slightly warm, but not hot. The onion mixture can be made 2 days in advance, then covered and refrigerated. Allow the onion mixture to come to room temperature before filling the dough and baking.

Evenly spread the onion mixture over the baked tart shell. Place the onion tart in the oven for 12 minutes to set the mixture, then place under the broiler for 2 to 3 minutes, just until the top becomes golden brown.

Using the parchment, remove the tart from the baking dish. The dough is brittle, so use a sawing motion to cut the tart into twenty-four two-bite pieces.

Tiramisu is Italian for "little pick-me-up." This fun dessert puts a tiramisu twist on a chocolate-covered strawberry, a longtime Champagne companion. Filled with sweet mascarpone cheese, like that used in the traditional Italian dessert, these strawberries are then dipped in chocolate to make a decadent, delicious sweet finale for this year of wine club.

Strawberries Tiramisu

Line a baking sheet with parchment or wax paper.

Using a small, sharp knife remove a small circle from the bottom tip of the strawberries. Keep the green stem end intact. Hollow out the center.

In a small bowl, stir together the mascarpone cheese and confectioners' sugar. Place into a piping bag with a small round tip. Pipe the cheese into the center of the strawberries.

Melt the chocolate in a double boiler. Holding the strawberry by the stem, dip into the melted chocolate and let the excess chocolate drip off. Place the dipped strawberries on the prepared baking sheet. Place in the refrigerator until ready to serve.

MAKES 12 PIECES

12 large sweet strawberries

1/2 cup [120 g] mascarpone cheese

2 tsp confectioners' sugar, sifted

3 oz [85 g] dark chocolate, chopped

Note: If you don't have a piping bag and a few tips, I encourage you to buy them. You can find them in most grocery stores or online. They make hors d'oeuvres so much cuter. And having the right tool for the job is much easier than wrangling with a plastic zip-top bag.

Acknowledgments

One page isn't enough to express how sincerely grateful I am to every person who touches my life, but I'll give it a whirl.

First, to my hubs, Michael: Thank you for all the support and patience, and for unflaggingly trusting the process. You are some kind of secret superhero. You have all my love, always.

There's no book without the people around me who support and love me, and in this case, love wine club. This idea started twenty years ago, with the OG Wine Club inspired by my friends in Atlanta—Vanessa, Tamie, Sarah, Susie, and Gil—who first let me write about wine. For you, all my wine-loving friends, and the dozens of wine clubs still going strong coast to coast, I hope you devour this one too.

To my fabulous editor and friend, Cristina Garces, and my super-agent, Sally Ekus, for bringing the band back together: I can write with ease knowing that Sally and Jaimee Constantine at the Ekus Group have my back. CG, there is no editor more skilled or as much fun in the whole world, and you have a critical eye Tim Gunn would kill for.

To Lizzie Vaughan, for your inspired art direction and design, and for bringing me the immensely talented illustrator Liv Lee. Thank you for the life you brought to these pages. Wine Club is more fun because of you. And to the rest of the dedicated and hardworking team at Chronicle: Tera Killip, Jessica Ling, Dena Rayess, Samantha Simon, Keely Thomas-Menter, and Gabby Vanacore. Thank you!

To my media faves and friends who have let me share my food and lifestyle ideas on air: My work wouldn't reach half as many fans without you, and I'm forever grateful. Rainy Farrell and Susan Durrwachter, you've been there since my very first Today show appearance a million years ago. Thanks to JoAnn La Marca for giving the original Wine Club its very first segment, and Tammy Filler for supporting the many more that followed! Thanks also to Sarah Clagett, my ride-or-die on all things lifestyle; Jackie Olensky, someone who's always up for a clink; Adam Miller, for inventing the title "Lifestyle Expert"; and Randi Fisch and Jamie Nguyen most recently for making my ideas come to life on screen. You are all TV magic.

To my creative circle and the people who always inspire me, believe in me, and push me to work hard: Shannon O'Neil, for reminding me daily to remember the important things and believe in myself. Amy Goodman, Jessica Downey, Belinda Morrison, and Kate Underwood for encouraging me and my work without fail. My OG Slack Tide crew, Chris, Jac, Scrappy, Lee Lee, and Claudia, for keeping me strong in more ways than you know. To my teammates on Fusion and the Delavue Manor Book/Wine Club: My world wouldn't be complete without you. And, of course, Amy Lynn, for all your sprinkles of joy and beauty.

Mom and Dad, I hope you're not tired of me dedicating books to you yet; I've got a couple more in me. Col, Dave, Christie, Daisy, Sean, Maeve, J, and Brenna, thanks fam for all the book love. To the Jersey Petroskys: I couldn't have better in-laws. Thank you all.

My scoops, Chris and Elliot: You continue to amaze me. I'm so excited to see what's next for you—go run the world.

Clink!
Maureen

Index